TASTING HISTORY

EXPLORE *the* PAST THROUGH
4,000 YEARS *of* RECIPES

TASTING
HISTORY

Max Miller
with Ann Volkwein

Photography by Andrew Bui

SIMON ELEMENT

NEW YORK   LONDON   TORONTO   SYDNEY   NEW DELHI

SIMON ELEMENT

An Imprint of Simon & Schuster, Inc.
1230 Avenue of the Americas
New York, NY 10020

First Simon Element hardcover edition April 2023

SIMON ELEMENT is a trademark of Simon & Schuster, Inc.

For information about special discounts for bulk purchases, please contact Simon & Schuster Special Sales at 1-866-506-1949 or business@simonandschuster.com.

The Simon & Schuster Speakers Bureau can bring authors to your live event. For more information or to book an event, contact the Simon & Schuster Speakers Bureau at 1-866-248-3049 or visit our website at www.simonspeakers.com.

Interior design by Matt Ryan
Photography by Andrew Bui
Food stylist: Max Rappaport
Food styling assistant: Elizabeth Katona
Prop stylist: Casha Doemland

Manufactured in the United States of America

13

Library of Congress Cataloging-in-Publication Data has been applied for.

ISBN 978-1-9821-8618-0
ISBN 978-1-9821-8619-7 (ebook)

For José and his endless patience

CONTENTS

This cookbook, and indeed my entire career, exists because my friend Maureen became terribly ill on vacation.

Let me explain. It was December 2015, and we were at Walt Disney World. We had planned to do all of the wonderful things that one does at Walt Disney World, but on the first day of our trip, Maureen came down with a miserable cold, and we spent the majority of the time in the hotel room eating too many nachos and watching TV. As we sat in bed in the darkened hotel room, Maureen introduced me to a show from England that she thought I, a devout Anglophile, would enjoy. And so we binged an entire season of *The Great British Bake Off* and my life was changed forever.

At that time, I had no interest nor experience in the kitchen. My then roommate still likes to remind me that I was unable to boil pasta water without his assistance; it was rather pathetic. But watching Mary Berry explain the subtle art of baking intrigued me, and I took the bakers' various failures as a personal challenge. On top of that, the hosts, Mel and Sue, would routinely step away from the tent to tell the audience about the history of whatever the bakers were baking, and for me, history has always been an ingredient to make any subject more enjoyable.

Five years and many baking mishaps later (I once used rose oil instead of rosewater in a pie, turning the apartment into a massive bowl of potpourri) and I had become quite the home baker. I was working at Walt Disney Studios in a job that I loved, and every Monday I would share my latest cake or pastry with my coworkers and it was always accompanied by a history. Whether it

was out of a genuine desire to see me share the information with a larger audience or if it was merely as a way to redirect the lectures away from them, one of them encouraged me to take my interests in food and history and unleash them on YouTube.

I knew immediately how I wanted to format the show. In the years since I'd first watched *The Great British Bake Off* in the sick room at Disney's Coronado Springs Resort, Mary Berry, Mel, and Sue had all left the show, as had the history lessons, and I missed them all. While Mary, Mel, and Sue were unlikely to join me in my kitchen, the history lessons were something I could bring back, and even expand. So, in February 2020, I started *Tasting History with Max Miller* on YouTube. A week later COVID-19 hit, movie theaters shut down, and I was furloughed from my job. Over the next few months, people all over the world hunkered down in their homes and became obsessed with making sourdough bread, and I, grateful for a distraction, was there to teach them its history. Though it was not sourdough, but *garum*, a fermented fish sauce from Ancient Rome and something I wouldn't encourage anyone to make at home, that really made the channel take off.

So had my friend not become horribly sick on vacation and had a global pandemic not seen me furloughed from a job that I loved, you wouldn't be holding this cookbook and I would still be using my oven to store old magazines. It just goes to show, you just never know what lies ahead.

They say "history is written by the victors," but in my experience, history is written by those who write stuff down, and food is no exception.

Of the innumerable dishes that humans have eaten throughout history, we know of only a fraction, and it's because somebody took the time to record the recipe. And recipes, like descriptions of past events, run the gamut from a comprehensive list of ingredients, precise measurements, and well-written cooking processes to a vague description of a dish mentioning only a couple of the ingredients. Spoiler: most recipes before 1850 find themselves on the latter end of that spectrum, but that's where this book comes in.

This is a book of modern recipes with precise measurements, cook times, and instructions, but for the most part, those specifics are of my own invention. Accompanying each modern recipe that you can easily make at home is the original historic recipe on which it's based. The goal has been to bring those original recipes back to life, to rekindle history in your kitchen, but that's often easier said than done. The frustration I feel when confronted with the enigmatic "salt to taste" in a modern recipe is a hundredfold when I read "put in good things and cook until it is enough" in a medieval recipe.

For most of history, recipes were written by cooks, for cooks, and so anyone reading it would know what those "good things" were and what "enough" was. To cause added confusion, those answers likely changed from cook to cook and year to year. Unfortunately, I don't always have the luxury of knowing what a cook in Renaissance Italy or sixteenth-century China knew, and so I make an educated guess by looking at other, better-written recipes of the period or even consulting later or modern recipes for solutions. Sometimes I also have to accept that I don't know the answer, and I never will know, and I just take a stab in the dark or else abandon the recipe altogether. In any case, re-creating historic recipes is always a series of educated guesses, some more informed than others, and because of that, my re-creations won't be the same as someone else's. As I've given the original recipe along with a modern version, you can be like that historic cook with the freedom to change things if you wish.

Historic cooking, at least in this book, is less a matter of academia and more a matter of fun. As a child, I loved pretending, imagining what it might be like to be a knight in medieval England or a gladiator in Ancient Rome, and while I rarely run around the house hacking at my family with a wooden sword these days, I never lost the passion for putting myself in the shoes of those who came before me. I've found the easiest and most delicious way to do so is by following their recipes and trying to eat what they ate. Though, once I put myself in the shoes of an eighteenth-century home cook whipping Everlasting Syllabub for thirty minutes, I realized that was a horribly inefficient way of doing things when I had an electric stand mixer three feet away. So, while doing my best to preserve the nature of each recipe, I've also optimized them for the modern kitchen, making it all the easier for you to make them yourself.

A Note on Ingredients

The hardest part about re-creating historic cuisine is finding the ingredients. Frankly, with few exceptions, it's impossible to find almost any of them. Modern farming and growing practices have altered everything from chickens to wheat to carrots to pretty much every ingredient there is. And while it's interesting for scholars to debate what a carrot in the court of Charlemagne might have tasted like, for our purposes it does not do to dwell on it. That said, there are some ingredients that, while not common in today's kitchen cupboard, add depth to many of the dishes in this cookbook and so are worth finding when possible.

Ale Barm: Barm is the yeasty foam that forms on the top of a fermenting liquid such as beer or ale and was a common form of yeast used to leaven bread from the Middle Ages through the nineteenth century. I have opted to use dried yeast for most every recipe that requires it, but if you have easy access to a brewer, barm is worth the effort when making the mead recipe, though even then, it is not necessary.

Asafetida (Asafoetida): Still used in Indian cuisine under the name *hing*, this ingredient is infamous for its pungent odor, which transforms to a smooth leek and garlic flavor during the cooking process. It was used during the Roman Empire as a replacement for the famous ingredient silphium, which was thought to have gone extinct in the first century. Asafetida is an ingredient that cannot be replicated and is worth the purchase either online or at an Indian market. Just make sure to keep it tightly closed and store it in a sealed plastic bag, or even two.

Currants: Few ingredients cause such consternation as currants due to two different ingredients sharing the same name. Today "currants" often refers to black or red berries used in jams, but in historic recipes it typically means Corinth raisins, which are one of the oldest varieties of raisin in the world. They originated in Greece and many came from the city of Corinth, and the name eventually became corrupted to the word "currant." Their other name is Zante currant, coming from the Greek isle of Zakynthos (Zante). Anywhere that currants are called for in this book, you should use the tiny raisin-like currant rather than the berry.

Defrutum: A reduction of grape must used in Ancient Roman cooking. It is very sweet and nearly as thick as syrup. Modern versions called *mosto cotto* or *saba* can be found online. You can also reduce ⅓ cup (80 ml) grape juice to 1 tablespoon for a similar, if less complex, ingredient.

Galangal: Galangal is a root in the ginger family and offers a sweet, woody flavor to many medieval dishes. It can often be found online either dried and sliced or in powder. The slices can be ground using a cheese grater. Common ginger will work as a substitute.

Garum: This ingredient is a must for nearly every Ancient Roman recipe. It's a fermented fish sauce that was often used in place of salt, but its flavor cannot be compared to salt and cannot be reproduced by anything other than fermented fish sauce. Luckily, any Asian market will have fish sauce, and online you can find modern Italian and Spanish versions such as Colatura di Alici and Matiz Flor de Garum.

Grains of paradise: Grains of paradise is a complex, aromatic spice popular in historic recipes. They offer the heat of black pepper with a hint of citrus and sweet ginger and cardamom. Their flavor is hard to replicate, though equal amounts of black pepper, ginger, and cardamom will come close.

Hyssop: A popular medieval herb still commonly used in tea, hyssop has a flavor that is a combination of mint and anise. Finding it in a tea bag is the easiest way of procuring this herb, as it's rarely sold fresh, but replacing it with mint and a pinch of powdered anise will serve as well.

Jaggery: Jaggery is a form of cane sugar or palm sap that is most common in Asian and African cuisine. Its flavor is less sweet and more bitter than white or brown sugar. It comes in solid blocks or cones and can be found in many Indian or Asian markets as well as Latin American markets under the name panela or piloncillo.

Long pepper: Long pepper is a spice popular throughout history, only losing favor in recent centuries when black pepper came to dominate Western cuisine. It has a similar flavor to black peppercorn but with a bit more heat and a lot more complexity. It truly is superior to black peppercorn in every way except in its availability at the grocery store. You'll likely have to get it online, but once you do you may find yourself filling your pepper mill with these instead of the classic peppercorn.

Lovage: A mildly sweet herb used in ancient and medieval cooking, lovage can be found in some gardens but is not common today and, like rue, has been used as an abortifacient. Celery leaf can be used as a substitute.

Passum: Used in many Ancient Roman recipes, *passum* was a wine made from semi-dried grapes; a raisin wine. It is very sweet and can be replaced by sweet wines such as Vin Santo or ice wine. For a less expensive alternative, a sweet Riesling or Moscato will do the trick.

Persian shallots: These are often dried and can be rehydrated in a bowl of water after a half hour. Their flavor is more akin to strong garlic than to a shallot.

Rue: An herb with a musty, bitter flavor used in ancient and medieval cooking, today rue is most often found in a dried form. In small quantities it is harmless but in large quantities can be toxic and an abortifacient. Parsley leaf can be used as a substitute.

Sandalwood powder: Sandalwood was used to color food red in the Middle Ages, though today it is more often used in cosmetics. As it is all but flavorless, a drop of red food coloring can be used instead.

Savory: Savory is an herb common in historic recipes and comes in two varieties, summer and winter. Recipes rarely call for either specifically, so it is chef's choice. Both varieties offer a robust and peppery taste to a dish—the summer variety has a tinge of heat that the earthier winter variety does not, though winter savory carries a hint of pine that is uncommon in foods today. The complex flavor of both varieties is hard to replicate, but using a combination of thyme and sage will work in a pinch.

Spikenard: Also called nard, this ingredient comes in several forms. The most common is as an oil and is not safe for use in food. The dried root can be used in food and lends a sweet, earthy flavor. As it is difficult to find as well as grind into a powder, it is an ingredient that can be left out of most recipes, as it is usually one of many herbs and spices used.

Tequesquite: Tequesquite is a natural salt mineral mined from several lakes in the State of Mexico. It usually contains sodium chloride and sodium carbonate and was used by the Aztecs as both a flavoring and leavening agent.

The

ANCIENT
WORLD

✳

Stew of Lamb

✖✖✖✖✖✖✖✖✖✖✖✖✖✖✖

City/Region: Babylon
Time Period: c. 1740 BC

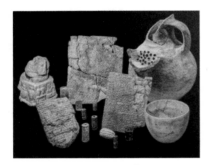

The Yale Babylonian Tablets and cooking utensils

This flavorful broth, which is more of a stew, stars one of Ancient Babylon's most loved ingredients: lamb. It also likely included the fat from a fat-tailed sheep, which are exactly what their name would imply. My favorite description of these animals was written by Herodotus in the fifth century BC:

They have . . . the tail long, not less than three cubits in length; and if one should allow them to drag these after them, they would have sores from their tails being worn away against the ground; but as it is, every one of the shepherds knows enough of carpentering to make little cars, which they tie under the tails, fastening the tail of each animal to a separate little car.

The fat from these tails is prized even today, as it tends to be less greasy than most other animal fat. Unfortunately, finding it can prove rather difficult, so we will use a different type of fat and rely on the meat to do the heavy lifting. Another feature of the stew is a crouton-like crunch that comes from crumbled *risnātu*. This is one of those words that have no definite translation, but it's generally agreed to be a sort of dried barley cake. It pairs well with the lamb, though, according to the Sumerian creation myth, the two ingredients haven't always gotten along so well.

At the beginning of the world, people on earth, on the one hand, had no bread, meat, or clothes and went around naked eating grass and drinking water from ditches. The Anuna, or great gods, on the other hand, sat on the Holy Mound where heaven and earth met having great feasts and generally living it up. For one feast the Anuna decided to create Sheep and Grain, but

A seventeenth-century depiction of a fat-tailed sheep

after a few bites the Anuna were not impressed, so they gave them to the gods Enki and Enlil to take down to the humans instead. The humans, used to eating grass, were less picky and loved the new ingredients, which they used not only for food but also to make beer, clothes, and even weapons. All was well, until Sheep and Grain sat down to dinner themselves and got a little tipsy on wine.

Grain boasts that she is superior to Sheep and that the humans love her more. But Sheep reminded Grain that it is she who is more loved by humans, as she provides the leather on which kings emboss their emblems. They also use her to make slings and quivers for arrows for protection. They use her stomach to hold water and her skin to make sandals. But Grain gave Sheep a knowing smile and said, "Beer. I make beer." One might think that was the trump card, but Sheep counters with ability to provide meat. Back and forth they go, neither giving in until finally they ask Enki and Enlil to settle the matter. I wish I could tell you that the gods told Sheep and Grain that they loved them equally and that they should get along as sisters, but that's not what happened. Enki says that, of the two of them, Grain is greater and Sheep should fall on her knees and praise her sister from sunrise to sunset.

Sumerian mythology is full of these debates between two related subjects: bird versus fish, summer versus winter, silver versus copper. With all of this conflict, it warms my heart to find a recipe where two of the combatants can come together and share a pot.

continues

Stew of Lamb

continued

FOR THE *RISNĀTU*:

1 cup (140 g) barley flour

½ teaspoon sea salt

⅓ cup (75 ml) water

¼ cup (60 ml) extra-virgin olive oil

FOR THE STEW:
Extra-virgin olive oil for cooking the onion

1 large onion, diced

¼ cup (50 g) rendered sheep fat or extra-virgin olive oil

1 pound (450 g) lamb, cut into large, bite-size pieces

2 teaspoons sea salt, divided

1 quart (1 liter) very hot water

¼ cup (50 g) chopped Persian shallot (see Cook's Note and page 13)

2 cups (475 ml) sheep milk (goat or cow milk will work as a substitute)

4 to 5 cloves garlic

½ cup chopped leek, plus more for garnish

1. Preheat the oven to 425°F/220°C.

2. Make the *risnātu*: Whisk together the barley flour and salt, then add the water and olive oil and mix into a ragged dough. Do not knead the dough. Form it into cakes several inches across and as thin as possible without them falling apart, about ¼ inch thick. Set them on a lined baking sheet and bake for 25 minutes, then turn off the oven, but leave the cakes in the oven to cool. This should dry out the cakes so they will easily crumble. Once they have dried, crush two-thirds into small crumbs and one-third into large, crouton-sized pieces.

3. Make the stew: Add a little olive oil to a pan and cook the diced onion, stirring frequently, until it starts to brown, about 7 minutes. Meanwhile, melt 1 tablespoon of the sheep fat or olive oil in a large pot over high heat, then add the lamb and sprinkle with 1 teaspoon of the salt. Sear the lamb until it begins to brown, then pour the hot water over the meat and add the rest of the salt and fat. Bring it to a boil, then lower the heat to medium low and let it simmer, uncovered, for 5 minutes. Then add the cooked onion, the Persian shallot, the milk, and the small *risnātu* crumbs, saving the larger pieces for later. Mix the stew and let it simmer for another 20 minutes.

4. While the stew simmers, grind the garlic in a mortar until it's a paste, then add the leek and grind it with the garlic, though the mixture will not become a paste. Stir the mixture into the simmering stew. At the end of the 20 minutes, if the stew has thickened more than you'd like, add more milk. It is up to you how much broth you'd like. Then cover the pot and let it simmer for another 20 to 30 minutes or until the lamb is very tender. Serve the dish with the large *risnātu* croutons on top and garnish with more chopped leek.

Cook's Note: Persian shallot often is sold dried and should be rehydrated in water for 30 minutes before measuring.

Tuh'u

City/Region: Babylon
Time Period: c. 1740 BC

> ## FROM HISTORY
>
> *Tuh'u. Lamb leg meat is used. You prepare water. You add fat. You sear. You fold in salt, beer, onion, arugula, cilantro, samīdu, cumin, and red? beet, and you crush leek and garlic. You sprinkle coriander on top. You add šuhutinnū and fresh cilantro.*
>
> —The Yale Babylonian Tablets
> (translation from Barjamovic et al., 2019)[1]

Tuh'u is one of the many recipes found in the Yale Babylonian Tablets. It's a beet and lamb stew that, while four thousand years old, is as complex as any stew made today. Lamb being a rather expensive ingredient, about one shekel of silver each, this dish was probably served at festivals. Perhaps the Akitu festival, which took place during the spring equinox. It was a time to celebrate the prime god Marduk's victory over Tiamat, Mother of Dragons and the goddess of the primordial sea.

> *He shot an arrow which pierced her belly,*
> *Split her down the middle and slit her heart,*
> *Vanquished her and extinguished her life.*
> *He threw down her corpse and stood on top of her.*
> *When he had slain Tiamat, the leader,*
> *He broke up her regiments; her assembly was scattered.*
> . . .
> *The gang of demons who all marched on her right,*
> *He fixed them with nose-ropes and tied their arms.*
> *He trampled their battle-filth beneath him.*
> . . .
> *The Lord trampled the lower part of Tiamat,*
> *With his unsparing mace smashed her skull,*
> *Severed the arteries of her blood,*
> *And made the North Wind carry it off as good news.*
> —*The Epic of Creation*[2]

continues

Tuh'u

continued

Marduk then used her body parts to create the world; her ribs held up the heavens and her weeping eyes watered the Tigris and Euphrates rivers. The brutality really makes you wonder who the good guy in the story is. Even the Babylonian king wanted to make sure to keep on Marduk's good side, which is essentially what the Akitu festival was all about.

To keep in the god's good graces, it took some assistance from the Šeš-gallu, or high priest of Marduk's Temple, the Ésagila. The king would humble himself by removing his crown and laying down his royal scepter. Then the Šešgallu would grab the king's ear and yank him to his knees and follow that up with a good, hard slap across the face. And I mean hard. There needed to be tears. If the king didn't cry, that was a sign that Marduk was less than thrilled, and nobody wants that. So if I were the king, I'd make sure to practice my Meryl Streep–esque crying on command before heading to the temple, because if the king let the tears flow, that meant Marduk was happy and the god would agree to let the king stay in power for another year. This is a tradition I believe we should reinstate for our political leaders.

Left: The Babylonian god Marduk

Right: Yale Babylonian Tablet

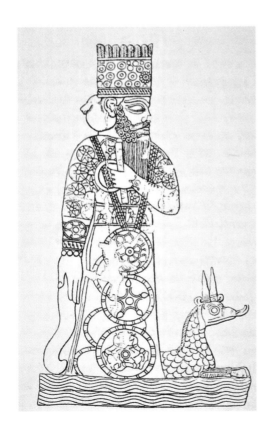

MAKES 8 TO 10 SERVINGS   **COOK TIME:** 1 HOUR 50 MINUTES

4 tablespoons extra-virgin
olive oil

1 pound (450 g) leg of lamb
chopped into bite-size pieces

1 large yellow onion, chopped

2 or 3 large red or golden beets,
chopped (approximately 4 cups)

12 ounces (350 ml) sour beer (it is
important that this is not a hoppy
beer like an IPA)

2 cups chopped arugula

¾ cup fresh cilantro leaves, finely
chopped, plus more for garnish

1 Persian shallot, chopped
(*samīdu*) (see page 13)

2 teaspoons ground cumin

1½ teaspoons sea salt

3 cloves garlic

1 large leek, finely chopped
(approximately 1½ cups)

2 cups (475 ml) water, as needed

1 tablespoon dry coriander seeds

1 cup Egyptian leek for garnish
(*šuhutinnū*)

1. Add the oil to a large pot and set over high heat. Add the lamb to the pot and sear for several minutes in the oil, turning the pieces several times until lightly browned on all sides. Stir in the onion and cook for 5 minutes. Add the beets and let cook for 5 minutes, stirring frequently. Add the beer, arugula, cilantro, shallot, cumin, and salt to the pot and bring to a boil.

2. Crush the garlic into a paste and mix with the leek, then add to the pot.

3. Lower the heat to medium and allow the stew to simmer for 60 to 90 minutes or until the beets and meat are cooked to your liking. As it simmers, add water when needed. The thickness of the stew is subjective, so the full 2 cups may not be needed.

4. Once the stew is cooked, ladle it into a bowl and sprinkle with coriander seeds. These can be crushed, though the whole seed will add a crunchy texture, which is most welcome. Garnish with fresh cilantro and chopped Egyptian leek.

History Facts: The words *samīdu* and *šuhutinnū* have no definite translation. *Šuhutinnū* is some sort of root vegetable and *samīdu* has been translated as both a type of shallot, leek, or root vegetable as well as a type of flour like semolina. Nobody knows, so you can make your own choice. For the sake of flavor, I've chosen to use the shallot, as it improves the flavor the most.

A lamb cost about one shekel of silver, or the same as one hundred loaves of bread, so while *tuh'u*'s not an inexpensive dish, it would be within reach of much of the population at least a few times a year.

Tiger Nut Cake

City/Region: Egypt
Time Period: c. 1400 BC

Opposite: Making tiger nut cakes, as depicted in the Tomb of Rekhmire. Reproduced by Nina de Garis Davies.

Most recipes are written with words, but this recipe for tiger nut cake is shown in pictures. On the walls of the Tomb of Rekhmire, a vizier, or chief adviser, to the pharaohs Thutmose III and Amenhotep II during the Eighteenth Dynasty, each step of the process is shown, from the crushing of tiger nuts to the final shaping of the cakes, but as they are only images, much is left to interpretation. It's clear that fat is used, but what kind? The liquid used to form the cakes has been guessed to be water, milk, or beer. And the cooking process is anything but definite. One ingredient that is clear is honey, as one panel depicts a man harvesting honey as another smokes the bees with a three-wick lamp, but it's not clear how this honey is used in the cakes. Another question is: What gives the cakes their dark color? Some have interpreted the image of a possible plate of dates as an ingredient to make date syrup to be drizzled over the cake, but who knows? Nobody. Only the role of the main ingredient, the tiger nuts, is clear.

Tiger nuts were used for all sorts of things in Ancient Egypt and were precious enough to be counted by the vizier himself. The Greek historian Theophrastus wrote of this most interesting of tubers:

> *In sandy places which are not far from the river, there grows underground the thing called malinathalle [tiger nuts]. . . . These, the people of Egypt collect and boil in beer made from barley, and they become extremely sweet, and they are used as sweet fruits.*
> —Theophrastus, *Historia Plantarum* 4.8.12

With these tiger nuts carrying the dish, everything else in this recipe is my best guess, but whether or not it's exactly what Rekhmire would have known, it is at least on the right track, as it makes a sweet confection that would be welcome on the table of any Egyptian vizier.

continues

Tiger Nut Cake

continued

4 cups (500 g) tiger nuts

1 cup (325 g) honey

⅓ cup (80 ml) warm water

½ cup (100 g) ghee or
extra-virgin olive oil

1 cup (325 g) date syrup,
if desired

MAKES 1 LARGE CAKE   **COOK TIME:** 1½ HOURS

1. First make a flour from the tiger nuts. You can buy tiger nut flour, but the consistency is quite different from that of flour you make—though you'll be forgiven for saving some time. First, soak the tiger nuts in warm water for 1 hour. Drain them and use a mallet to break them into large pieces, to grind more efficiently in the food processor. Grind the broken tiger nuts in a food processor until you have a coarse flour. It is easiest if you do this in small batches rather than adding all of the tiger nuts at once.

2. Combine the flour with honey in a large bowl until just incorporated, then add the warm water, one tablespoon at a time, until it comes together like a dough. Note that you may not need the entire ⅓ cup of water, though you may need more.

3. Add the ghee or olive oil to a pan set over medium heat and warm it just enough to melt the ghee or cover the bottom of the pan. Add the tiger nut dough and cook for 4 to 5 minutes, or until it starts to smell toasted. Keep the dough moving around the pan with a spoon the entire time to prevent burning.

4. Once it's toasted, set the dough on a large piece of aluminum foil and spread it out to let it cool for about 10 minutes, or until it's cool enough to touch with your hands. Form the dough into a large cone on its side, ensuring that there is a flat base so it can stand. Then cover lightly with foil and put it in the refrigerator to firm up before serving.

5. The tiger nut cake can be presented standing on end but should be served lying on its side, with a drizzle of date syrup, if desired.

Kykeon

✕✕✕✕✕✕✕✕✕✕✕✕✕✕

City/Region: Ancient Greece
Time Period: c. 700 BC

Circe Offering the Cup to Odysseus by John William Waterhouse

Kykeon is not a particularly appetizing concoction, nor is it meant to be, for *kykeon* is a magic potion from Ancient Greece. It was a key component of the Eleusinian Mysteries, ancient initiation rites for the cult of Demeter and Persephone held at the Sanctuary of Eleusis. During a portion of the ceremony called the Telesterion, the initiates, following a long fast, would be given *kykeon* laced with pennyroyal and possibly psychotropics, thus letting them commune with the gods. It's possible that these drugs were similar to the wicked poisons the witch Circe adds to the *kykeon* offered to Odysseus's men just before she turns them into pigs.

But *kykeon* wasn't always used for ill. In another Homeric description from *The Iliad*, the poet describes a *kykeon* prepared by captive Hecamede made for King Nestor and Machaon to heal their wounds from battle. Hers is accompanied by onion relish and is sprinkled with goat's cheese grated on a bronze grater.

Each description of *kykeon* has a slightly different preparation as well as various additives, but they all share three ingredients: barley, cheese, and Pramnian wine. The first two are simple enough to procure, but you may be hard-pressed to find a bottle of Pramnian wine at your local liquor store.

Pramnian wine was first produced on the slopes of Mount Pramnos on the isle of Ikaria. The grapes were said to be a gift from Dionysus himself and the wine, rather than drunk for pleasure or quenching thirst, was a "fat and strengthening" medicine in and of itself. The Greek grammarian Hesychius called it a praiseworthy yet hard wine and the playwright Aristophanes said

that Athenians stayed well away from the stuff, as it made both their eyebrows and stomachs contract. With that in mind, it may be a good thing that it's not readily available to use in the recipe here and we'll have to be content with any dry red wine.

MAKES 4 SERVINGS   **COOK TIME:** 1 HOUR 40 MINUTES

2 cups (300 g) hulled barley

Dry red wine

Honey

Aged hard goat cheese

1. Set the hulled barley in a dry pan and place over medium heat. Stirring frequently, let the barley toast until it becomes aromatic, 7 to 10 minutes. Using a mortar and pestle, coarsely grind the barley. Fill a medium saucepan with water and bring to a boil, then add the barley and boil, until the barley is very soft, like a porridge, 1 hour to 90 minutes. Then drain the water.

2. Spoon the barley porridge into a bowl or cup and pour some wine over it, mixing until it has a drinkable consistency. Add a spoonful of honey and mix until smooth. Grate the goat cheese over the top and enjoy.

Melas Zomos (Spartan Black Broth)

City/Region: Sparta
Time Period: c. 400 BC

This Spartan broth that Plutarch writes of is the infamous Melas Zomos. And while antiquity leaves no recipe, it's described as a black broth made with pork eaten by Spartan warriors as part of their daily meal, or *aiklon*, that took place in the Syssitia, which was similar to a military mess hall. The *aiklon* was basic. Spartan, even.

> *The dinner is at first served separately to each member, and there is no sharing of any kind with one's neighbor. Afterwards there is a barley-cake as large as each desires, and for drinking, a cup is set beside him to use whenever he is thirsty. The same meat dish is given to all on every occasion, a piece of boiled pork. . . . Besides this there is nothing whatsoever, except, of course the broth made from this meat. There may possibly be an olive or a cheese or a fig . . . or something similar.*
> —Athenaeus, the *Deipnosophistae*[2]

But after the *aiklon* came the *epaikla*, a sort of potluck where they brought food made at home. They ate *kammata*, which were cakes made with barley meal soaked in olive oil and wrapped in laurel leaves. They also ate fresh greens, wheat bread, beans, sausage, and little round honey cakes called *physikillos*. But it was the Melas Zomos that non-Spartan Greeks made infamous in their writings. In the *Deipnosophistae*, Athenaeus tells of a man from Sybaris who dined in Sparta and subsequently proclaimed:

continues

Melas Zomos (Spartan Black Broth)

continued

It is no wonder that Spartans are the bravest men in the world; for anyone in his right mind would prefer to die ten thousand times rather than [live as miserably as this.][5]

I won't think less of you if you should pass over this recipe. But if you do have the fortitude to try it (and I promise you, actually it tastes quite good), know that you are one step closer to being a Spartan warrior.

MAKES 8 SERVINGS **COOK TIME:** 1½ HOURS

4 tablespoons (60 ml) extra-virgin olive oil, divided

1 large white onion, finely chopped

2 pounds (900 g) pork shoulder, cut into 1-inch squares

1 teaspoon kosher salt

1 teaspoon freshly ground black pepper

3 bay leaves

3 cups (710 ml) water

1 cup (235 ml) white wine vinegar

2 cups (475 ml) pork blood

1. Heat 2 tablespoons of olive oil in a medium skillet over medium-high heat; add the onion. Cook, stirring frequently, until it becomes tender and browned, about 10 minutes.

2. Heat the remaining 2 tablespoons of olive oil in a large pot over medium-high heat and add the pork. Season with salt and pepper, then brown the meat on all sides, about 3 minutes. Add the cooked onion, bay leaves, water, and vinegar and raise the heat to high to bring to a boil. Once the soup is boiling, reduce the heat and simmer, covered, until the pork is tender, about 45 minutes.

3. While the soup cooks, make sure the pork blood is fully liquified. If you have purchased a brick of coagulated blood, put it in a blender with 1 cup (235 ml) of water and blend until liquid. Strain the pork blood through a strainer and remove any solids, then add the blood to the soup and continue to simmer for at least 15 minutes.

Pottery depicting Greek hoplites in battle

Epityrum

City/Region:
The Roman Republic
Time Period: c. 160 BC

FROM HISTORY

Epityrum is prepared this way. Select some green, black and mottled olives and remove the pits. Chop them up fine. Add a dressing of oil, vinegar, coriander, cumin, fennel, rue, and mint. Cover with oil in an earthenware dish, and serve.

—Cato the Elder, *De agri cultura* 119[1]

With the possible exception of grapes, olives are the most important ingredient in the cuisines of Ancient Greece and Rome, and perhaps modern Greece and Rome as well. Olive oil is used in almost every ancient recipe, yet few use the actual fruit. This recipe for an olive relish, however, uses both.

According to Greek mythology, olives were a gift from the goddess Athena. King Kekrops founded a city atop the Acropolis rock that he called Attica. To be taken seriously, Attica needed a patron god and so they held auditions. The two contenders were Poseidon, god of the sea, and Athena, goddess of wisdom among other things. Each god made a gift to the city in the hope of winning the job as patron. Poseidon took his trident and smashed it into the Acropolis rock and up bubbled a spring—though, as he was the god of the sea, it was salt water. Athena, much more practical, took her spear and thrust it into the ground, from which grew the first olive tree. King Kekrops declared a winner and Attica became known as Athens: good news for the Greek board of tourism, as "Poseidonopolis" just doesn't roll off the tongue.

Athena's tree and any that sprouted from its olive seeds were considered sacred. Even if one was on your land, it was illegal to chop it down. The Greek logographer Lysias (c. 445–c. 380 BCE) wrote a speech for an accused man to defend himself for just such a crime in front of the boule, which was a deliberative body of five hundred citizens that ran the day-to-day of Athenian Democracy. Sadly, we do not know the outcome of the trial, but

continues

Epityrum

continued

if he was found guilty, hopefully he wasn't too severely punished, as these Athenian olives grew like gangbusters.

Herodotus tells the story that Xerxes brought the Persian army into Athens and burned the Temple of Athena along with her original olive tree. Feeling guilty, or perhaps fearful of the goddess's wrath, he ordered some Athenians to return the next day with offerings to her to try to smooth things over. But when they went into the burnt temple, they found the tree had already grown back a full cubit, or a half meter, overnight. No harm, no foul. All the same, as you make your *epityrum*, I'd make sure to offer a little prayer of thanks to Athena.

MAKES ABOUT 2 CUPS **COOK TIME:** 5 MINUTES

1½ tablespoons finely chopped fresh cilantro

1½ tablespoons chopped fresh fennel leaf

1½ tablespoons chopped fresh mint

2 teaspoons chopped rue, fresh or dried (see Cook's Note and page 13)

1 teaspoon ground cumin

2 tablespoons (30 ml) red wine vinegar

¼ cup (60 ml) extra-virgin olive oil, plus more for drizzling

2 cups (300 g) pitted, brined green and black olives (such as Cretan green or Kalamata black olives)

Mild goat cheese and bread with an optional drizzle of olive oil

Mix the cilantro, fennel, mint, rue, and cumin in a small bowl. Pour the vinegar and oil over the herbs and mix well. Lightly rinse the olives in cool water, but do not soak. Pat the olives dry, then finely chop for a relish or mash for a more spreadable tapenade. Add the olives to the herbs and mix until combined. Cover and let marinate overnight, though the flavor will improve if left to marinate for several days. Serve with a mild goat cheese and bread with an optional drizzle of olive oil.

Cook's Note: While rarely a problem, rue can be considered unsafe if you are pregnant. Omit or replace with another herb, such as fresh tarragon.

Globi

City/Region:
The Roman Republic
Time Period: c. 160 BC

Dice players from a wall painting in Pompeii

I think of *globi* as an early form of cheesecake bites, the kind you might find on a tray at a holiday party. And that's exactly when you might have found them in Ancient Rome as well. One such holiday was Saturnalia. For a few wonderful days each December, Romans would remove the trappings of their rigid class system and party down.

You are indeed a reckless lad,
At Saturn's feast in toga clad!
—*Martial: The Twelve Books of Epigrams*[2]

The togas of the elite were swapped out for more casual attire like the Greek synthesis, which I equate to an ancient Hawaiian shirt: casual and colorful, but able to be dressed up with a nice pair of slacks. People also donned the *pilleus*, which was a conical felt cap worn by freed slaves. Once everyone was dressed the same, more or less, it was time for gambling, feasting, and gift giving.

Gambling was illegal most of the year, but as the fourth-century Calendar of Philocalus says, during Saturnalia, "Now, slave, you are free to play with your master." It was also a time slaves could eat with their master. There were even stories of the tables being turned and the masters serving the slaves. Ancient Roman Opposite Day!

But the best part of Saturnalia, in my opinion, had to be the gifts. For most people, these would be small wax or clay figurines called *sigillaria*, but if you were friends with the emperor you could often count on something a little more spectacular . . . sometimes not.

On the Saturnalia, [Emperor Augustus] would now give gifts of clothing or gold or silver . . . another time nothing but hair cloth, sponges, pokers and tongs, and other such things under misleading names of double meaning.
—Suetonius, *The Life of Augustus* 75

With the gift giving and feasting in December, the festival definitely hints at the later Christmas holiday, and just as Christmas has its Ebenezer Scrooge, so did Saturnalia have Pliny the Younger:

I find it delightful to sit there, especially during the Saturnalia, when all the rest of the house rings with merriment and shouts of the festival-makers; for then I do not interfere with their amusements, and they do not distract me from my studies.
—Pliny the Younger, *Letter to Gallus*

Bah! Humbug.

MAKES 20 TO 24 *GLOBI*   **COOK TIME:** 30 MINUTES

1 cup and 1 tablespoon (120 g) spelt, durum, or other whole-grain flour

1 cup (240 g) ricotta cheese

1 teaspoon sea salt

1 quart (1 liter) of extra-virgin olive oil

⅓ cup (80 ml) honey

1 tablespoon poppy seeds

1. Mix the flour, cheese, and salt in a large bowl until well combined.

2. Form the mixture into balls 1 inch across. This recipe should make 20 to 24 balls.

3. Pour the oil into a medium saucepan and place over a high heat until it reaches 325°F (165°C).

4. Once the oil reaches the desired temperature, turn heat down to medium and carefully place 2 to 3 balls in at a time, turning every 10 to 15 seconds with metal tongs. At 60 seconds, begin to check the color. Once they are a golden brown (60 to 90 seconds) take them out and set them on a wire rack over paper towels to drain. Repeat until all of the *globi* are fried.

5. Once the *globi* are drained, dip them in honey (heating the honey can help if it is too thick). Then sprinkle or coat with poppy seeds and serve warm.

Placenta

City/Region:
The Roman Republic
Time Period: c. 160 BC

A marble bust thought to be
Cato the Elder

When you think "placenta," the last thing you're probably thinking about is cake, but that's essentially what the word means. This placenta is a layered honey and cheese cake from Ancient Rome and its shape is thought to have inspired the anatomical term "placenta," though I assure you this one is more appetizing.

The recipe comes from the treatise *De agri cultura*, or *On Agriculture*, by Marcus Porcius Cato (c. 234 BC–149 BC). Cato the Elder, as he is more commonly called, was a conservative statesman known for his hatred of everything not Roman. He detested the influence Greek culture had on the Roman people and above all he had a lifelong loathing of Carthage in northern Africa. While I disagree with his hatred of Greek culture, his hatred of Carthage is understandable.

As a young man he was pulled off the farm that he loved when Hannibal Barca invaded the Italian peninsula with a massive army and a few surviving elephants, most of which had died after crossing the Alps. Turns out elephants don't do well in weather conditions normally saved for skiing trips. Cato distinguished himself during the war, but while the Carthaginians lost, he was never convinced they were truly defeated. He became famous, and was sometimes ridiculed, in the Roman Senate for ending every speech with the phrase *Carthago delenda est!* (Carthage must be destroyed!).

But it isn't his hatred of Carthage or Greek culture that makes him important to the lover of historical food, but rather his fondness for farming. Much of what we know about Roman food and farming practices comes from his writings. In *De agri cultura* he tells the reader not only how to farm but also how to do so profitably. Sometimes this included best practices of how to grow crops and which crops made the most money or which blessings to perform to ensure that the gods allowed your farm to keep running. Though sometimes the advice was far less charming, like how to reduce rations for slaves if they weren't working hard enough and advice on selling those slaves if they got sick or too old to work. But regardless of our modern feelings on Cato's business practices, we can thank his writings for giving us not only this recipe but also a glimpse into the values of the average Roman citizen at the time. "When they would praise a worthy man, their praise took this form: 'Good husbandman, good farmer'; . . . it is from the farming class that the bravest men and the sturdiest soldiers come."[2]

continues

Placenta

continued

FOR THE TRACTA:
⅔ cup (120 g) whole spelt or emmer

1 cup (235 ml) water

2 cups (240 g) all-purpose flour

Extra-virgin olive oil

FOR THE FILLING:
1¾ pounds (790 g) feta cheese

¾ cup (255 g) honey, plus more for coating

FOR THE CRUST:
¾ cup (175 ml) water

1½ cups (180 g) all-purpose flour

12 to 15 fresh bay leaves coated in extra-virgin olive oil

1. Make the *tracta*: Grind the whole spelt or emmer in a mortar until they are coarsely ground. Put them in a small bowl and add 1 cup of water. Cover and leave to soak for 24 hours.

2. Once they are soaked, mix them, and any water left, with flour in a medium bowl to form a dough. If a dough does not form, add more water, 1 tablespoon at a time, until it comes together. Turn the dough out onto a lightly oiled surface, and knead until it becomes smooth, then divide into six pieces and let rest, lightly covered, for 20 minutes. Roll each piece into a thin disk, 8 inches across. Make them as thin as possible, similar to tortillas. They can be slightly smaller than 8 inches, but no larger. Make sure they are all the same size and discard any extra dough. Set the disks on a baking sheet and leave out to dry until leather-hard, 4 to 6 hours. Do not let them dry too much or they will begin to deform, making the final product hard to assemble.

3. Preheat the oven to 300°F/150°C.

4. Make the filling: Break the cheese up into chunks in a large bowl and cover it in water, rinsing as much salt out of the cheese as possible. Then set it in a strainer and press out as much liquid as you can. If you have a very salty cheese, repeat this process up to three times, but for most cheeses, once will be adequate. In a clean bowl, press the cheese with your hands until it is as smooth as possible, then add the honey and, using a spatula, mix until well incorporated. Set aside while you prepare the crust.

5. Make the crust: Add ¾ cup water to the flour and work it in with your hands until it makes a dough. Knead the dough by hand for 5 minutes, then form it into a ball and cover, letting it rest for 20 minutes. Then roll on a lightly oiled surface into a disk as thin and large as possible while still holding together.

6. To bake the placenta, the best baking vessel is a ceramic casserole dish with a lid that is slightly larger than the size of the *tracta*, about 9 inches. A shallow pot with a lid will work as well. Line the bottom of the dish with oiled bay leaves, then set the dough for the crust on top of the leaves, letting the additional crust hang over the sides of the dish. Lightly brush olive oil on both sides of one of the dried *tracta* and place it in the center of the dish on top of the crust. Take ⅓ of the filling and spread it evenly over the *tracta*. Layer another oiled *tracta* on top of the filling and repeat until all of the filling is used and the fourth oiled *tracta* is set on top. Then wrap the crust up and over the placenta, encasing it as much as possible. It is okay if some of the *tracta* remains uncovered, as long as the crust is secure and will not slip down the side during baking. Cover the dish with the lid and bake for 1 hour and 10 minutes. Remove the lid from the dish and allow the placenta to bake for 10 more minutes. Then remove the dish from the oven and use a spatula to remove the placenta, setting it on a serving plate. Immediately drizzle honey all over the top, letting it run down the sides. Serve warm.

Roman harvesting machine

Puls

City/Region:
The Roman Empire
Time Period: c. 2nd century

FROM HISTORY

*There is also much use made of fava beans . . .
Our gladiators eat a great deal of this food
every day, making the condition of their body
fleshy—not compact, dense flesh like pork,
but flesh that is somehow more flabby.*

—Galen[1]

T his is a classic *puls*, or porridge, the staple of the Ancient Roman diet. There were many variations on the dish, most being rather simple but filling, and this one, gleaned from the writings of Galen, physician to the gladiators of Pergamon, is no exception. Galen says that the fava beans, which he complains caused excessive flatulence, were a main ingredient in what the poet Juvenal called "the hotchpotch of the gladiator."

Depending on time and location, the gladiator's diet may have included some variety of fish or meat, but the bulk of the diet was typically grain heavy. Pliny the Elder says the fighters were once called *hordearii*, literally meaning "barley men." Between the beans and barley, it's no wonder that in reality there was a softness surrounding those rippling muscles of the gladiator depicted in movies. Though when you spend the day being slashed at with swords or spears, a little natural padding might not be a bad thing.

For a full banquet of meats, cheese, wine, and other assorted goodies, the average gladiator might have to wait for the Cena Libera, a feast eaten the night before a bout in the arena. It was usually a public spectacle meant to entice an audience to attend the games the following day, though some sources claim most gladiators would rather spend time with family or put their affairs in order instead of gorging themselves just before a big fight. For our purposes, we'll stick to the barley and beans.

MAKES 4 SERVINGS   **COOK TIME:** 1 HOUR 15 MINUTES

1 cup (150 g) dried fava beans

1 cup (170 g) hulled barley

3 tablespoons (45 ml) extra-virgin olive oil

1 large onion, chopped

1 quart (1 liter) water

3 cloves garlic, pressed

2 tablespoons (30 ml) red wine vinegar

2 teaspoons *garum* (see page 12) or Asian fish sauce

1. In separate bowls, soak the fava beans and barley in cool water for 12 hours, then drain and peel the fava beans, discarding the skins.

2. Heat the olive oil in a medium pot over medium heat. Add the onion and cook until translucent, about 5 minutes. Pour the quart of water into the pot and bring to a boil. Add the barley and cover the pot, boiling for 30 minutes.

3. Add the fava beans, garlic, vinegar, and *garum*, and stir until combined. Bring to a simmer and allow the *puls* to cook down, uncovered, into a thick porridge, about 30 minutes.

History Fact: Gladiators were often the entertainment at the banquets of Rome's elite, and "often the combatants fell dead above the very cups of the revellers, and the tables were stained with streams of blood."[2]

Police Verso by Jean-Léon Gérôme

In Mitulis (Mussels)

City/Region:
The Roman Empire
Time Period:
c. 1st to 4th century

Roman fresco depicting a banquet scene from Pompeii

We can't cover Ancient Roman cooking without talking about *Apicius*. The vast majority of Ancient Roman recipes comes from this, the only true Roman cookbook. Officially, it's called *De re coquinaria*, or *On the Subject of Cooking*, but it is often called simply *Apicius*, because even though the recipes span several centuries, they're all attributed to one man, Rome's most famous gourmand, Marcus Gavius Apicius.

Living during the reign of Tiberius (14 BC to 38 BC), Apicius was infamous for his lavish dinner parties where Rome's elite would gather to feast on the most expensive and outlandish dishes, some of which are featured in *De re coquinaria*: sow's udder stuffed with sea urchins, roast flamingo, and dormouse stuffed with pork and silphium (an ingredient so precious it will get a full explanation in the next recipe). When it came to dictating what was and was not acceptable to eat for the upper class, Apicius's word was practically law. He convinced Drusus, the son of Emperor Tiberius, to shun cabbage sprouts and cabbage tops, as they were fit only for the common folk, and instead urged his guests toward flamingo tongue or pork liver from a pig fed on the finest dried figs and made to get drunk on honeyed wine on its way to slaughter.

Drunk pigs aside, Apicius was on a never-ending quest to procure the most exotic and spectacular ingredients for his dinners. On one occasion, upon hearing a boast of the biggest and sweetest shrimp being caught on the Libyan coast, he hired a boat to sail him across the Mediterranean Sea only to take one unimpressed look at the shrimp, tut, and sail back to Italy without ever stepping ashore. But like the social media influencers of today who flex beyond their means, the gourmand of Ancient Rome's spending habits finally caught up with him as well:

continues

In Mitulis
(Mussels)

continued

After he had spent a hundred million sesterces on his kitchen, and had wasted on each single banquet a sum equal to so many presents from the reigning emperors . . . he then for the first time was forced to examine his accounts: he calculated that he would have ten million left of his fortune, and, as though he would live a life of mere starvation on ten million, put an end to his life by poison.

—Seneca, "On Consolation to Helvia"

While I decided not to include any of the recipes for flamingo tongue or drunken pig, namely because those ingredients are very hard to source, I have included several other recipes from Apicius, including this simple, yet unique, recipe for mussels.

MAKES 2 POUNDS OF MUSSELS   **COOK TIME:** 15 MINUTES

2 pounds (1 kg) live mussels

1 large leek, chopped into rounds

¾ cup (180 ml) water

¼ cup (60 ml) dry white wine

2 tablespoons (30 ml) Vin Santo or fortified sweet wine

1 tablespoon (15 ml) *garum* (see page 12) or other fish sauce

¼ teaspoon ground cumin

½ teaspoon dried or 1½ teaspoons minced fresh savory (see page 13)

1. Wash the mussels under running water and inspect each to make sure they are firmly closed. Discard any that are open. Scrub the shells and pull off any hairlike "beards" sprouting from the shell.

2. Add leek, water, white wine, Vin Santo, *garum*, cumin, and savory to a large pot and stir to combine. There should be at least ½ inch of liquid at the bottom of the pot. If there is less, add more water or more wine. Set the pot over medium-high heat and bring to a simmer. Add the mussels to the pot, cover, and steam until the majority of the mussels have opened, 6 to 8 minutes. Remove the pot from the heat and discard any mussels that have not opened. Serve the others with a bit of the broth in which they steamed.

History Facts: One of the earliest existing copies of *De re coquinaria* is a tiny, abbreviated version, titled *Apici excerpta a Vinidario,* or *An Abridged Apicius by Vinidarius.*

Like many premodern cookbooks, *De re coquinaria* includes several medicinal recipes. One, preventing general illness, calls for stinging nettles gathered when the sun is in the sign of Aries.

Patina de Piris (Patina of Pears)

City/Region:
The Roman Empire
Time Period:
c. 1st to 4th century

Fruit basket with vases from Pompeii

This recipe is essentially a sweet frittata and would fall under the category of dessert in Ancient Rome. Though while the pear and honey do make it sweet, it's not anything you'd expect to be served after a meal today, because even if you could accept the presence of cumin and pepper in a dessert, the addition of *garum*, also known as *liquamen*, would likely have you opt for the safer choice of chocolate ice cream. *Garum* is fermented fish sauce and was a beloved ingredient in Ancient Rome, often being a substitute for salt, just as it is today in many East Asian cuisines.

Made from fish, usually tuna or mackerel, salt, and herbs, *garum* was big business all across the Mediterranean. Pliny the Elder called it "choice liquor" and preferred a type from southern Spain called *garum sociorum*, or *"garum* of comrades," and claimed that no liquid but perfume was more highly valued. *Garum* was prized both as an ingredient and as a medicine. Pliny claimed it could treat dog bites and earaches. If you had an attack of collywobbles, then an odd number of African snails marinated in *garum* would set you right in no time. (I'm assuming an even number would produce the opposite effect.) And Pliny wasn't alone in his praise of *garum* as medicine, for the Greek physician Galen claimed it could treat ulcers and, if taken as an enema, alleviate sciatica. Let's all take a moment and appreciate modern medicine.

The problem with *garum* is in its production. Huge vats of fermenting fish sitting out in the hot Mediterranean sun created a stench that seemed to wreak havoc on real estate values. In some places, it was so bad that laws, like those in the Byzantine *Hexabiblos*, stated that any new *garum* factories had to be built far from any city or town. Another issue with *garum*

continues

Patina de Piris (Patina of Pears)

continued

seemed to be its aftereffects. Multiple writers tell about the putrid belching of those who enjoyed too much *garum* and the poet Martial once praised a young man for being able to continue his romantic advances on a woman after she'd had six helpings of *garum*. With that in mind, we'll go light on the *garum* in this recipe and I think you'll find that there is no fishy flavor, but simply a savory umami, a flavor that is hard to put into words but is intrinsic to Roman cuisine. Just to be safe, you may want to wait a few hours before kissing anyone.

MAKES 4 SERVINGS   **COOK TIME:** 1 HOUR

1 bottle (750 ml) sweet white wine

4 medium firm, ripe pears

2 tablespoons (30 ml) honey

Pinch of freshly ground black pepper, plus more if desired for garnish

Pinch of ground cumin

4 large eggs

½ cup (120 ml) sweet dessert wine

1 tablespoon (15 ml) *garum* (see page 12) or other fish sauce

1 tablespoon (15 ml) extra-virgin olive oil

1. Pour the bottle of white wine in a large saucepan and add enough water that you will be able to easily submerge the pears. Heat the wine and water on the stove to a low boil. Peel and core the pears, cut them in half, then submerge the halves in the wine. Simmer until cooked through, 10 to 15 minutes. Every few minutes, push the pears down with a spoon making sure they remain fully submerged. You'll know they're cooked when you can easily insert a paring knife through the pears with no resistance. Carefully remove the pears from the pan and puree them by hand or in a food processor with the honey, pepper, and cumin. Let the mixture cool to room temperature.

2. Preheat the oven to 350°F/175°C.

3. Once the mixture is cooled, add the eggs, dessert wine, *garum*, and olive oil and mix or blend everything into a smooth filling.

4. Lightly grease a small casserole dish with olive oil. Pour the filling into the dish and bake for 20 minutes or until the patina is set in the middle. Remove from the oven and serve immediately—garnished with freshly ground black pepper, if desired.

Sauce with Herbs for Fried Fish

XXXXXXXXXXXXXXXXXX

City/Region:
The Roman Empire
Time Period:
c. 1st to 4th century

> ### FROM HISTORY
>
> *Sauce with herbs for Fried Fish: Take any fish you like, clean, salt, fry. Pound pepper, cumin, coriander seed, silphium root, oregano, rue; pound well, moisten with vinegar, add dates, honey, defrutum, oil, garum. Mix all in a pot to let it boil. Once boiling, pour it over the fried fish. Sprinkle with pepper and serve.*
>
> —Apicius, *De re coquinaria*

A fifth-century depiction of Dido and Aeneas reclining during dinner

This sweet and herbaceous sauce, which Apicius says is for fried fish, is really perfect on almost anything. That may be because it's made with one of Ancient Rome's most prized ingredients: silphium. The only problem is, according to Pliny the Elder, silphium is extinct, the last stalk eaten by the Emperor Nero. Some believe the plant still grows wild in North Africa, but if it does its identity is unknown to us today. Luckily, after Nero finished it off, the Romans found a suitable alternative called asafetida, which came from the Parthian Empire to the east (see recipe for Parthian Chicken, page 53), and so that is what we'll use for our recipe. But when it comes to the original brand-name ingredient:

> *We find it stated by the most trustworthy among the Greek writers, that this plant first made its appearance in the vicinity of the gardens of the Hesperides and the Greater Syrtis, immediately after the earth had been soaked by a rain, black as pitch. This took place seven years before the foundation of the city of Cyrenae, and in the year of Rome 143.*
> —Pliny the Elder, *The Natural History*

continues

Sauce with Herbs for Fried Fish

continued

Cyrenae was located along the coast of modern-day Libya, and the city made its fortune by exporting silphium to Egypt, Greece, and Rome where "the Dictator Caesar, at the beginning of the Civil War, took from out of the public treasury, besides gold and silver, no less than fifteen hundred pounds of laserpicium (silphium sap)."

And perhaps it was the flavor that put it on par with gold and silver, but it may have also had to do with its many medicinal uses. Pliny says it could be used to raise the body temperature of someone suffering from hypothermia, treat corns on the feet, act as a digestive and diuretic, neutralize snake venom, and treat gout, pleurisy, quinsy, sciatica, and epilepsy. While it may seem like a cure-all, Pliny warns:

For my own part, I should not recommend, what some authors advise, to insert a pill of laser, covered with wax, in a hollow tooth, for toothache; being warned to the contrary by a remarkable case of a man, who, after doing so, threw himself headlong from the top of a house. Besides, it is a well-known fact, that if it is rubbed on the muzzle of a bull, it irritates him to an extraordinary degree; and that if it is mixed with wine, it will cause serpents to burst—those reptiles being extremely fond of wine.

Medical uses alone might explain the worth of this precious ingredient, but as it also had a reputation as an aphrodisiac and a contraceptive, one can see why the Roman treasury kept it stockpiled. Unfortunately, I cannot claim that the substitute, asafetida, will make you amorous or ease your gout, but I can promise, the flavor will not disappoint.

continues

A coin of Magas and Cyrene showing a silphium plant and crabs

Sauce with Herbs for Fried Fish

continued

1 whole fish (approximately 1½ pounds) or 1 pound of filet

1 teaspoon sea salt

3 tablespoons (45 ml) red wine vinegar

2 tablespoons (30 ml) honey

2 tablespoons (30 ml) extra-virgin olive oil, plus more for frying

1 tablespoon (15 ml) *mosto cotto* or ⅓ cup grape juice reduced to 1 tablespoon

1 tablespoon (15 ml) *garum* (see page 12) or other fish sauce

3 dates, pitted and minced

1 teaspoon minced fresh oregano

½ teaspoon freshly ground black pepper

½ teaspoon ground cumin

½ teaspoon ground coriander

½ teaspoon asafetida powder (see page 12)

½ teaspoon dried rue (see page 13)

MAKES 1 WHOLE FISH WITH SAUCE FOR 2 SERVINGS
COOK TIME: 20 MINUTES

1. Clean and gut the fish, then make several shallow diagonal slices on each side and season the entire fish with salt, making sure to get inside the slices. Set the fish aside while you prepare the sauce.

2. In a small saucepan, stir together the red wine vinegar, honey, olive oil, *mosto cotto*, and *garum*. Stir in the dates, oregano, pepper, cumin, coriander, asafetida, and dried rue. Set over medium heat and bring to a simmer. Simmer for 2 minutes, then lower the heat to keep it warm while you fry the fish.

3. Add ½ inch oil to a skillet and heat it over high heat until very hot (400°F/205°C). Reduce heat to medium and carefully set the fish in the oil. Fry on one side, undisturbed, for 4 to 5 minutes. Do not move the fish once it is in the skillet or it will fall apart. After 4 minutes, test to see if the fish is cooked by attempting to lift it with a fish spatula. If it feels stuck to the skillet, continue to let it cook for another minute. Then, gently flip and fry the other side for the same amount of time. When cooked, remove the fish from the skillet and place on a wire rack set over a paper towel to drain. Once it is drained, plate the fish and pour the sauce over the top, and serve.

History Fact: There is speculation that silphium's heart-shaped seed pod and the plant's link to romance may be the inspiration for our modern heart-shaped symbol of love.

Pullum Parthicum (Parthian Chicken)

✕✕✕✕✕✕✕✕✕✕✕✕✕

City/Region:
The Roman Empire
Time Period:
c. 1st to 4th century

> ### FROM HISTORY
>
> *Parthian Chicken: Open the chicken and quarter. Pound pepper, lovage, a little caraway, moisten with garum, season with wine. Arrange the chicken in an earthen dish and put the seasoning on top. Dissolve silphium in warm water, and put it with the chicken and cook. Sprinkle pepper and serve.*
>
> —Apicius, *De re coquinaria*

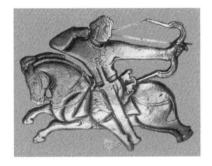

Relief from the Hephthalite silver bowl depicting a Parthian Shot

Pullum Parthicum is a Roman recipe, but it takes its name from the Parthian Empire, a sometime trading partner, sometime mortal enemy of Rome. The Parthian Empire ruled over modern-day Afghanistan, Iran, and Iraq from 247 BC to AD 224, setting them smack dab in the middle of the Silk Road, which ran from China to Rome. With such a choice spot on the map of Asia, they became the greatest middlemen in history (in addition to their formidable army and lasting effects on the culture of the Middle East, of course).

From Rome came gold, silver, perfumes, glass, and cloth made from asbestos. Yes, that stuff in the walls of my childhood home that was supposed to stick in my lungs and kill me before I reached thirty. I'm still kickin'! The cloth seems to have been used as a novelty item. In a story of the sixth-century Sasanian king Khosrow II, he liked to impress dinner guests by cleaning his asbestos dinner napkin by lighting it on fire!

The Chinese mostly sent back jade, spices, and silk. But they also imported silk from Rome. They would send Rome thick brocade made of the stuff and then the Romans would unravel it and reweave it into a lighter textile like the silk cloth we know today. But the Parthians, ever business minded, let China believe that Rome's silk was brand-new, made from Roman silkworms (which did not exist). That kept the Chinese from knowing they had a monopoly on the thread, which kept the price down. Parthia knew they couldn't let their trading partners speak to one another lest

continues

Pullum Parthicum (Parthian Chicken)

continued

the jig be up. "You want silk? You want glass? You gotta go through me." They were so adept at controlling the conversation that in the entire four-hundred-year history of the Han Dynasty in China, only one person was ever recorded as having been able to "cut out the middleman."

According to the *Hou Hanshu*, a fifth-century chronicle of the Han Dynasty, in the year 97 the great general Ban Chao sent Gan Ying as an ambassador to visit the far-off kingdom of Da Qin, which is what they called the Roman Empire. Somehow Gan Ying made it all the way across Parthia without being stopped until he reached the Persian Gulf. When he requested a ship to take him on to Rome, he was told: "The ocean is huge. . . . If you encounter winds that delay you, it can take two years. . . . The vast ocean urges men to think of their country, and get homesick, and some of them die."[1]

That was enough of a deterrent for Gan Ying, so he asked for a few secondhand accounts of Rome from the sailors and returned to China.

MAKES 4 SERVINGS   **COOK TIME:** 1 HOUR

1 (3- to 4-pound) (1.5 kg) whole chicken

1 cup (235 ml) dry red wine

3 tablespoons (45 ml) *garum* (see page 12) or Asian fish sauce

1 tablespoon dried lovage (see page 13) or celery leaf (or 2 tablespoons if using fresh leaves)

1½ teaspoons freshly ground black pepper, plus extra for garnish

1½ teaspoons ground caraway seeds

¾ teaspoon powdered asafetida (see page 12)

¼ cup (60 ml) lukewarm water

1. Preheat the oven to 450°F/230°C.

2. Quarter the chicken and place it in a single layer in an oven-safe dish. For a crispier skin, refrigerate covered in foil overnight, but this is not necessary.

3. Add the wine and *garum* to a medium bowl. Mix in the lovage, black pepper, and caraway seeds. Pour the mixture over the chicken, rubbing it to coat the skin.

4. In a small bowl mix the asafetida in the lukewarm water, and pour it over the chicken.

5. Place the dish on the middle oven rack and bake for 40 to 45 minutes or until an instant-read thermometer stuck in the breast measures 165°F/74°C.

6. When the chicken is cooked, remove the dish from the oven and allow the chicken to rest in the dish for 10 minutes. Then serve the chicken, drizzling the sauce in which it was cooked over it and sprinkling with ground pepper.

Vitellian Piglet

City/Region:
The Roman Empire
Time Period:
c. 1st to 4th century

There are several dishes named after the Emperor Vitellius, and this pork, with a sweet and spiced sauce, is my favorite. While the original recipe calls for a full pig, I've reduced the recipe for a more practical evening meal, but if you have a piglet on hand all you have to do is make more sauce. Though while Aulus Vitellius gets to have his name slapped on this and a number of famous Roman dishes, it's doubtful that it was because he had any particular fondness for them. More likely, they are an homage to an emperor associated with food and gluttony, as he hardly had enough time in power to accomplish much else.

The year AD 69 is known as the Year of Four Emperors, and Vitellius was number three. Following the death of Emperor Nero, the new emperor, Galba, sent Vitellius to command the army in Germania Inferior in the modern-day Netherlands. He did this not out of any respect for Vitellius's military prowess, but "since Galba openly declared that no men were less to be feared than those who thought of nothing but eating, and that Vitellius's bottomless gullet might be filled from the resources of the province, it is clear to anyone that he was chosen rather through contempt than favor" (Suetonius, *The Life of Vitellius*, 7).

But much to Galba's chagrin, Vitellius was incredibly popular with the army. So much so that they crowned him emperor and followed him back to Rome to overthrow Galba. But before they reached the city, Galba was murdered and a second emperor, Otho, took power. But one emperor was as good as another and Vitellius's armies defeated Otho at the Battle of Bedri-

continues

Vitellian Piglet

continued

Vitellius, emperor of Rome

acum and he entered Rome the triumphant third emperor of the year. While he was already known as a man with an epic appetite, his time at the top was where he really cemented the reputation:

> *He divided his feasts into three, sometimes into four a day; breakfast, luncheon, dinner, and a bout of drinking. And he was readily able to do justice to all of them through his habit of taking emetics.*

And Suetonius says that every day he ate a feast costing no less than 400,000 sesterces, somewhere between $200,000 and $800,000 today. One dinner, given by Vitellius's brother, included

> *two thousand of the choicest fishes and seven thousand birds . . . On a platter so large he called it the Shield of Minerva, Defender of the city . . . he mingled the livers of pike, the brains of pheasants and peacocks, the tongues of flamingoes and the milt of lampreys, brought by his captains and triremes from the whole empire, from Parthia to the Spanish straight.*

He also claimed that Vitellius,

> *being a man of an appetite that was not only boundless, but also regardless of time or decency, could never refrain, even when sacrificing . . . from snatching bits of meat and cakes amid the altars . . . and devouring them on the spot.*

Suetonius was clearly not a fan. So, he was probably not that upset when, after only a few months in power, Vitellius was removed from office following a short but bloody civil war with the fourth and final emperor that year, Vespasian. Vitellius was tortured and decapitated, his body thrown into the Tiber River and his head paraded around the city. A bloody end, but when it comes to posterity, it seems that food is where he is remembered.

> *All of the most costly viands were brought from afar . . . and were prepared in so costly a fashion that even now certain cakes and other dishes are named Vitellian, after him.*
> —Cassius Dio[1]

SERVES 8 TO 12   **COOK TIME:** 20 HOURS 30 MINUTES

1 (4- to 6-pound) (1.8 to 2.7 kg) bone-in pork butt (or similar cut)

Kosher salt

2 cups sweet white dessert wine (such as Moscato)

1 cup light white wine (such as pinot grigio)

3 tablespoons (45 ml) extra-virgin olive oil

2 tablespoons finely chopped fresh lovage (see page 13) or celery leaf

1½ tablespoons *garum* (see page 12) or Asian fish sauce

¼ teaspoon coarsely ground black pepper

1. Use a sharp knife to cut slits across the surface of the layer of fat on the pork, spaced 1 inch apart in a crosshatch pattern. Be sure not to cut into the meat. Rub salt over the entire roast, making sure to get into the slits you've cut. Wrap the roast in aluminum foil and refrigerate for 12 to 24 hours.

2. Preheat the oven to 250°F/120°C and adjust the oven rack to the lowest position.

3. Remove the pork from the refrigerator and let it rest for an hour, then set it, fatty side up, on a wire rack in a roasting pan. Roast the pork, uncovered, until a thermometer inserted in the thickest part of the roast registers 185°F/85°C, 6 to 8 hours depending on the oven and size of the roast. To achieve a proper reading, it is important not to let the thermometer touch the bone. Remove the pork from the oven, tent with aluminum foil, and allow it to rest for 30 minutes.

4. Make the sauce: Mix the dessert wine, white wine, olive oil, lovage, *garum*, and black pepper in a medium saucepan. Set it over medium heat and bring to a simmer. Allow to reduce to ⅓ of its original volume, about 30 minutes, occasionally stirring. Note that this will be a liquid sauce, similar to a vinaigrette, rather than a thickened sauce as is common today.

5. Remove the foil from the roast and pour half of the sauce over it, allowing it to get in the cracks on the fatty side of the roast. Reserve the remainder of the sauce to be served with the roast once carved.

History Fact: The oldest surviving manuscript of *Beowulf* is named "Cotton Vitellius A.XV" because it was kept in a bookcase that had the bust of Emperor Vitellius on it in Sir Robert Cotton's library.

The
BRITISH
ISLES
×•×

Mead

City/Region: England
Time Period: c. 1300

FROM HISTORY

*For to make mead. Take 1 gallon of fine honey
and to that 4 gallons of water and heat that
water till it be as lengh then dissolve the honey
in the water. then set them over the fire & let
them boil and ever scum it as long as any filth
riseth there on. and then take it down off the
fire and let it cool in another vessel till it be as
cold as milk when it cometh from the cow. then
take dregs of the finest ale or else barme and
cast it into the water & the honey. and stir all
well together but first look before thou put thy
barme in that the water with the honey be put in
a fair stand & then put in thy barme or else thy
dregs for that is best & stir well together/ and
lay straw or else cloth about the vessel & above
if the weather be cold and so let it stand 3 days
& nights if the weather be cold and if it be hot
weather 1 day and 1 night is enough at the full.
But ever after 1 hour or 2 at the most try thereof
and if thou wilt have it swete take it the sooner
from the dregs & if thou wilt have it sharp let
it stand the longer there with. Then draw it
from the dregs as clear as thou may in to
another vessel clean & let it stand 1 night
or 2 and then draw it into another clean
vessel and serve it forth.*

*And if you will make mead eglyn, take sage,
hyssop, rosemary, agrimony, saxifrage, betony,
centory, lunaria, harts tongue, thyme,
maribium album, Jon herb, of each a handful
if you make 12 gallons and if you make less
take the less of herbs, and to 4 gallons of
the matter, 1 gallon of dregs.*

—*Tractus Manuscript*: Folio 20R

Fourteenth-century depiction of beekeeping from *Tacuinum Sanitatis*

Mead can be as varied as wine and beer and has been made in almost every civilization that had access to honey. Ancient China, India, Greece, and Rome all praised what the *Rig-Veda* calls "our life-giver . . . the food to which all Deities and mortals, call meath" (*Rig-Veda*, Book 8, Hymn XLVIII).

This English recipe, written around 1300, is one of the simplest and fastest ways to make the drink and would have been what most mead drinkers would have had access to throughout the early Middle Ages. Very sweet, lightly alcoholic, and effervescent. The Welsh poem *Kanu y med*, or "Song of Mead," from AD 550, tells of this sparkling mead:

> *A giver of mead is Maelgwn of Mona, and at this mead-board*
> *His mead-horns circulate wine of the right colour.*
> *The bee has collected it and has not used it.*
> *For the distilling of the [sparkling] mead, praised be it above all.*

For the people of Northern Europe, mead was more than just an intoxicating beverage. It was used as a way to bestow favor and cement relationships, as Hrothgar, the king in *Beowulf*, does with his warriors in the mead hall, Heorot. That is, until Grendel comes and murders most of them.

Mead also appears in Northern European myths as something that magically bestows powers on those who drink it. Most notably in the Norse myth of the Mead of Poetry.

Following a war between the Norse gods, a truce was sealed by spitting into a cauldron. Makes sense. Out of the saliva of the gods sprung a being named Kvasir. A great poet and said to be the wisest of all men. Whenever in a bind, the gods depended on him for his knowledge of things. The Wikipedia of the Norse pantheon. When he wasn't needed, he would go to Midgard and share his knowledge with the humans and other creatures of the world.

One day, he met two dwarves, Fjalar and Galar, who bid him, "Come on in. We'll make you some mead." And they did. They made him some mead. They killed him, drained his blood into three containers, then mixed in honey, thereby creating the Mead of Poetry. Anyone who drank this mead would be given a bit of Kvasir's wisdom and a touch of his poetic talent. Unfortunately for Fjalar and Galar, they didn't hold on to the mead for long and all three containers ended up in the hands of a giant named Suttungr, where they caught the attention of the one and only Odin.

continues

Mead

continued

Odin, being Odin, tricked Suttungr into letting him have a sip from each of the three containers. As he was a god, Odin's sips were enough to drain the vats, after which he turned into an eagle and flew home to Asgard. There he threw the mead up into his own containers, presumably to save for a future poetry emergency, but in doing so he dribbled a bit back down to earth, giving rise to mediocre poetry.

MAKES 1 GALLON OF MEAD   **COOK TIME:** 5 TO 9 DAYS

1 gallon (4 liters) spring water

1 quart (3 pounds) (1 liter) raw honey (100 percent pure honey with no preservatives)

2 cups fresh herbs to make the mead "elgyn" (metheglin) (the recipe calls for numerous herbs, but the easiest to find are sage, rosemary, and thyme), optional

2 teaspoons ale barm (see page 12) or dry ale yeast

1 teaspoon yeast nutrient or booster (follow the directions on the nutrient or booster, as it may require less yeast be used), optional

1. Add the water to a large pot and heat over high heat until boiling. Remove the pot from the heat and immediately stir in the honey until dissolved.

2. Return the pot to the high heat and return to a boil, removing any scum that rises to the top. Most commercially bought honeys will not produce much scum. After 5 minutes of boiling, remove the pot from the heat and carefully pour mixture into a second clean pot or large jar. If you are using an earthenware jar to ferment the mead, then it is okay to pour the boiling liquid directly in. If you are using glass, then pour the liquid into another clean metal pot and wait until it has cooled before transferring to the glass vessel to prevent shattering. If you choose to make the mead "eglyn" by adding herbs, add them now and mix them in while the mead cools.

3. Allow the honey and water mixture to cool to 98°F/37°C. If you are using a glass vessel for fermenting, this is the time to transfer the liquid to that vessel. Then add the ale barm, or yeast, and yeast nutrient, if using, and stir until dissolved.

4. Cover loosely with aluminum foil or cloth and allow to sit, out of direct sunlight, for 3 to 7 days.

5. Next, transfer it to a bottle, trying to transfer as little of the yeast that has fallen to the bottom of the vessel. Fit an air lock into the bottle and add some water to the air lock to prevent dust from entering the bottle. Let sit, out of direct sunlight, for 2 nights.

Odin spits the Mead of
Poetry into several vessels
in this illustration by Jakob
Sigerðsson

6. At this point, the mead is ready to drink. It can be poured directly from the bottle or siphoned. If pouring, try not to disturb the lees (the yeast sediment at the bottom). These can be added to the next batch of mead, along with fresh yeast, to enhance the flavor.

Cook's Note: This recipe is for the quick, sweet, cloudy, low-alcohol mead that was common in the Middle Ages. To raise the alcohol level and temper the sweetness, you can allow it to ferment for longer; up to 3 months. At no point should the bottle be sealed, as the mead will still be fermenting and building up pressure.

Gingerbread

City/Region: England
Time Period: c. 14th century

Legend has it that gingerbread originally found its way to Europe in 992, by way of an Armenian monk named Gregory of Nicopolis. He brought a honey-and-spice cake to the monks of Bondaroy, France, where, upon tasting it, his guests believed it to be the food of heaven. Sounds like gingerbread to me, though it's possible that it contained no ginger at all and was what the French would later call *pain d'épices*, or spiced bread. Oddly, many medieval recipes for gingerbread include no ginger and the term was considered a catchall for any of the spiced breads popular in the courts of Europe. Even today, German pfefferkuchen, or pepper cake, rarely includes any pepper but does include ginger. It's all very confusing.

Early on, gingerbread was meant only for the elite. In "The Tale of Sir Thopas" in *The Canterbury Tales*, Geoffrey Chaucer lists gingerbread alongside the very expensive ingredients of cumin and sugar:

They brought him first the sweet wine.
And mead also in a maselyn
And royal spicery
Of gingerbread that was full fine,
And licorice, and also cumin,
With sugar that is nice.

Left: Sixteenth-century German inspecting molds for gingerbread

Right: Hansel and Gretel by Jenny Nyström

And in the thirteenth century, the monks of Nuremberg began baking a gingerbread called lebkuchen that was so precious in its ingredients and its creation that a guild was eventually established to regulate its production. Except at Christmas and Easter, only guild members were allowed to bake the precious treat.

According to lore, the Holy Roman Emperor Frederick III, in an effort to bolster his popularity, had four thousand of these lebkuchen molded into his likeness and given to the children of the city. Elizabeth I of England also liked having gingerbread made into human form, though instead of her own, she had them molded to depict visiting dignitaries and courtiers, and would give them as gifts. Thankfully, not long after the Virgin Queen died the price of gingerbread came down and small pieces were sold for a penny each at fairs throughout England.

As gingerbread became a treat for the masses, new recipes began to become a must in nearly every recipe of the eighteenth century. They would often have several recipes, from soft gingerbread cake to the hard gingerbread biscuit that would become a popular construction material following the success of the fairy tale "Hansel and Gretel" in the early nineteenth century. But this recipe for medieval gingerbread is nothing like either of those. While it includes actual bread as an ingredient, the finished product is closer to a chewy ginger candy with a potent ginger flavor meant for only the most ardent lovers of the root.

continues

Gingerbread

continued

MAKES 20 TO 25 1-INCH PIECES
COOK TIME: 2 HOURS 25 MINUTES

12 to 14 slices (238 g) stale white bread

1 cup (330 g) honey

1 tablespoon ground ginger

¾ teaspoon ground long pepper (see page 13)

½ teaspoon sandalwood powder, if desired, for color only (see page 13)

¼ cup (50 g) or less sugar (enough for sprinkling)

20 to 25 whole cloves

Gold leaf

1. Either with a food processor or by hand, grind the bread into coarse bread crumbs. Commercially bought bread crumbs will work as well, though the texture from homemade bread crumbs is preferable.

2. Pour the honey into a large saucepan set over medium heat, and heat to a rolling boil; the honey will become like syrup. Note that it will boil up quite a bit, so do not use a small saucepan. Slowly, add the bread crumbs to the honey while stirring. The mixture should come together and begin to pull away from the sides of the saucepan. Continue to mix until fully combined. Remove the pan from the heat and quickly stir in the ginger, long pepper, and sandalwood, if desired. Turn the mixture out onto a sheet of parchment and spread with a spatula. Then, place another sheet of parchment and, with a rolling pin, roll the gingerbread out to about ½ inch thick (1.25 cm). Wrap in plastic wrap and chill in the refrigerator until stiff, about 2 hours.

3. Once the gingerbread is cool, sprinkle sugar on top and cut into 1-inch squares or whatever shape you like. Keep in mind that each piece should be bite-size, as they are very strong. They will also be quite sticky, so handle them as little as possible. Insert a whole clove into each piece of gingerbread and fleck with gold leaf. Leave the clove in until serving, then remove it just before eating.

Douce Ame (Capon in Milk & Honey)

City/Region: England
Time Period: c. 1390

A sweetly sauced chicken dish from the fourteenth century, Douce Ame was originally meant to be made with a capon, which, according to the thirteenth-century scholar Bartholomaeus Anglicus, "is a cock made as it were female by carving away of his gendering stones." That is, a castrated rooster. Not very common today, capons often found their way into the cookbooks of medieval and Renaissance Europe, though their history goes back further than that.

Nobody knows who the first person was to neuter a rooster, but one story sets it during a drought in Ancient Rome in 162 BC. A set of laws called the *Lex Faunia* were passed that, among other things, forbade fattening hens, as it was seen as a waste of grain. Instead, it was found that castrating roosters would cause them to grow larger. This led to their being called capons, coming from the word *capo*, meaning "to cut."

The practice went out of fashion after the fall of the Western Roman Empire, but it came back in the Middle Ages and became associated with the wealthy and, in the case of Chaucer, friars. Chaucer often used rich foods to show the contempt he had for monks and friars, as when the Friar orders a large meal before claiming he doesn't eat much in "The Summoner's Tale":

Have I naught of a capon but the liver,
And of your soft bread naught but a sliver,
And after that a roasted pig's head
But that I need no beast for me were dead.

Then had I with you plain sufficience.
I am a man of little sustenance.

Shakespeare, too, associates the bird with the wealthy and gluttonous. The character Falstaff is particularly fond of the dish, and in *As You Like It* the Bard mentions it as a dish to be enjoyed during the fifth stage of life, when one should have amassed some wealth and wisdom:

And then the Justice
In fair round belly with good capon lined,
With eyes severe and beard of formal cut,
Full of wise saws and modern instances
And so he plays his part.

MAKES 4 SERVINGS   **COOK TIME:** 1 HOUR

---

2 to 3 pounds (1 to 1½ kg) chicken (or capon) cut into large pieces (legs and wings kept whole, breast and thigh cut in two or three pieces)

3 or 4 tablespoons extra-virgin olive oil or melted unsalted butter

2 cups (475 ml) whole milk

1 cup (235 ml) heavy whipping cream

⅓ cup (80 ml) honey

3 tablespoons chopped fresh parsley

3 tablespoons chopped fresh sage

3 tablespoons chopped fresh hyssop (see page 13) or mint

1 tablespoon dried savory (see page 13)

1½ teaspoons sea salt

Pinch of saffron

⅓ cup (50 g) pine nuts

1. Preheat the oven to 300°F/150°C.

2. Lightly coat the chicken in the olive oil or melted butter, then place the chicken, a few pieces at a time, in a skillet set over medium heat until lightly browned. Repeat until all the chicken is browned, then set aside, keeping any drippings in the pan.

3. In a small saucepan, combine the milk, cream, honey, parsley, sage, hyssop, savory, salt, and saffron and set over medium heat until simmering. Simmer for 5 minutes watching to make sure it does not boil. Add the pine nuts and the drippings from the pan the chicken was fried in, stir, and let simmer for 2 more minutes.

4. Layer the chicken in an oven-safe dish and pour the milk and honey mixture over it. Cover and set in the oven to cook for 30 minutes, or until the chicken is cooked through.

5. Remove from the oven and serve the chicken in the sauce.

Rapey

XXXXXXXXXXXXXXXXXX

City/Region: England
Time Period: c. 1390

Eighteenth-century depiction
of figs and leaves

This is a dish with an unfortunate name, but so delicious that it, nevertheless, demands a place in this book. Rapey is any kind of spiced fruit spread, and the star of the English recipe is the almighty fig. Figs are one of the oldest documented fruits. They were cultivated in Asia Minor as far back as eleven thousand years ago, and by 2500 BC the Sumerians wrote of figs being turned into cakes called *she-er-ku* that would be given as offerings to the gods. And figs must have enjoyed this association with the gods, as they continued to find their way into many of the old religions.

The Egyptian goddess Hathor was said to have sprung from a fig tree when she welcomed the souls of pharaohs to the afterlife. The Buddha, Siddhartha Gautama, sat under a fig tree, known as the Bodhi Tree, to attain enlightenment, and while I cannot say that it was the figs themselves that led to Buddha's awakening, it still looks good on their résumé. Even the prophet Mohammad once mused that the fig had come directly from Paradise. In Ancient Greece figs were given as prizes to Olympic winners, and in Rome they were eaten by those laid low by sickness or used as political pawns . . . let me explain.

Cato the Elder (see the recipe for placenta, page 38) had a lifelong hatred of the city of Carthage. When he was young, the Carthaginian Hannibal Barca had invaded the Italian peninsula and nearly conquered Rome. They were beaten back across the Mediterranean and many believed them to be vanquished. As the years passed, memory of the Second Punic War faded and the youngsters of the Roman Senate came to think of Carthage as a fallen power far across the sea, too distant to pose any real threat. But Cato remembered. He spent his last years trying to convince his fellow senators of the danger lurking on the coast of North Africa and finished every speech with the call to arms *Carthago delenda est!* (Carthage must be destroyed!). But it fell on deaf ears. Then one day, Cato bought some figs, tucked them into his toga, and during a speech in the senate casually dropped a few on the floor. The other senators marveled at how fresh and ripe the figs were and Cato laughed, triumphant. He pointed out that these figs were very fresh and they were picked only a few days before, on the Carthaginian coast. Thus, if figs can reach Rome in a few days, so, too, can the Carthaginian army. Not long after that, Rome fell upon Carthage in the Third Punic War, this time following Cato's call to action, and destroyed the city entirely.

By the medieval era, figs had lost their religious and political power but remained a much beloved fruit especially in Northern Europe, as, once dried, they kept for months and could be transported thousands of miles, as well as turned into the most delicious of dishes, such as our poorly named Rapey.

MAKES 2 CUPS   **COOK TIME:** 50 MINUTES

---

1 cup (150 g) stemmed and seeded, finely chopped figs

1 cup (160 g) dark raisins

1¼ cups (295 ml) light red wine

Pinch of freshly ground black pepper

½ teaspoon ground cinnamon

¼ teaspoon ground ginger

¼ teaspoon ground nutmeg

1 tablespoon rice flour

Pinch of sea salt

½ teaspoon sandalwood powder, if desired (see Cook's Note and page 13)

1. Soak the figs and raisins in cold water for 30 minutes, then drain them and put them in a small saucepan. Add the red wine, pepper, cinnamon, ginger, and nutmeg. Mix until combined, then cover the pot and bring to a light boil over medium-high heat for 10 minutes.

2. Once it is boiled, pour the Rapey into a blender and blend until smooth. There should be very little liquid remaining, but if there is, strain it through a sieve and return the mixture to the saucepan. Mix in the rice flour, salt, and sandalwood powder, if desired. Then place it on the stove and heat over low heat for 5 minutes or until any moisture has steamed off and the Rapey is thickened. Then serve it on bread or with cheese. It goes particularly well with the Tart de Bry (see page 74).

Cook's Note: Sandalwood powder is not easy to find and has no effect on the taste but was merely used to color the dish. In some dishes, it adds a vibrant red color, but as this is made with figs, raisins, and red wine, the effect is minimal, so feel free to leave it out.

Tart de Bry

City/Region: England
Time Period: c. 1390

M any a cheese has claimed the title King of Cheese, but for my part, Brie takes the crown, if for no other reason than it is the "Cheese of Kings."

According to legend, in 774 Charles I, the future Emperor Charlemagne, stopped in at the Priory of Reuil-en-Brie on his way home from defeating the Lombards. The abbot gave the king a bit of their cheese and he was so impressed that he decided to have two cartloads delivered to his palace in Aachen every year thereafter. As with so many things, Charlemagne set the trend when it came to cheese.

In 1217, King Philippe-Auguste gifted two hundred rounds of the cheese as New Year's gifts to the ladies of his court. Who doesn't appreciate a practical gift? Then, in 1594, Henry IV of France fell under the spell of Brie when he ate it at a supper with Queen Margot, one night at their castle in Meaux. Afterward, the queen would often request the cheese be served and the king, being an old romantic, was said to have only eaten with the queen, rather than with his mistress. These medieval kings clearly enjoyed their Brie, but one eighteenth-century king absolutely lost his head over it!

In June 1791, losing faith that the French Revolution would just blow over, Louis XVI decided to flee from the revolting peasants of Paris to the safety of his fortress in Montmédy, two hundred miles away. The royal family concocted a complicated escape plan that involved sneaking out from the Tuileries Palace through unguarded doors at midnight, changing clothes to disguise themselves as servants, using false passports and bodyguards to take a taxi carriage through the backstreets of Paris, then exchanging carriages outside the city and making a mad dash for the fortress. But the choreography went unrehearsed, and on the day of the show things didn't go well.

Before they even got to the carriage, Marie Antoinette got lost and spent several minutes wandering the streets outside the palace. When they eventually got underway, rather than being transported in a nondescript carriage that would allow them to blend in, they were ensconced in a conspicuous coach drawn by six horses. They soon came upon a wedding party that blocked the road and were forced to take a longer route out of Paris. Another hour was lost when the carriage broke down and a horse became unharnessed—and at several stops, Louis insisted on getting out to chat with peasants while the horses were being changed. Marie Antoinette, clueless as always, passed out silver dishes to local officials who had given them assistance.

Despite these delays and setbacks, they successfully made their way, seemingly undetected, to the town of Varennes, only twenty miles shy of their destination. And that is when King Louis, who I assume had been asking the coachman, "Are we there yet?" ever since leaving Paris, began to feel peckish for a bit of Brie cheese and a glass of Burgundy. They stopped at an inn to indulge. Different versions of the story abound, but they all agree that, at some point, the royal couple had indeed been recognized (perhaps because Louis's face was on the coins everyone was using) and had been pursued. This last pit stop was what allowed the revolutionaries to catch up to the royal entourage and, in the midst of their wine and Brie, they were all taken into custody and returned to Paris, where, after a couple years in captivity, Louis was marched up to Madame Guillotine. His last request? A final taste of Brie de Meaux.

With the French monarchy gone, the Cheese of Kings had to find a new champion. Enter Charles-Maurice de Talleyrand-Périgord, French diplomat and the man tasked with saving France's standing in Europe at the Congress of Vienna in 1815. This was just after the defeat of Napoleon at Waterloo, so he had his work cut out for him. But he had a card up his sleeve: Brie.

Via a series of opulent dinners, Talleyrand won over the leaders of Europe, and as the conference drew to a close he played his ace. In a display of gastronomic diplomacy, Talleyrand held a contest to determine the greatest cheese of Europe. Lord Castlereagh nominated English Stilton, Baron de Falck espoused Dutch Limburger, the Swiss had Gruyère, and Italy, Stracchino. Fifty-two cheeses in all were brought forth to the contest, the last being Talleyrand's own: a wheel of Brie de Meaux. And it was that Brie that helped France retain some of its pride as, via a vote by the other nations, it was crowned "Le Roi des Fromages." No longer just the Cheese of Kings, but the King of Cheese!

Fourteenth-century depiction of cheese-making from *Tacuinum Sanitatis*

continues

Tart de Bry

continued

MAKES ONE 9-INCH TART   **COOK TIME:** 2 HOURS

FOR THE CRUST:
½ cup (65 g) powdered sugar

½ cup (113 g) salted butter, chilled and cut into ½-inch cubes, plus more for greasing

3 or 4 large egg yolks

1¾ cups (238 g) all-purpose flour

FOR THE FILLING:
1 pound Brie cheese

6 large egg yolks, lightly beaten

½ teaspoon ground ginger

¼ cup (50 g) granulated sugar

Pinch of saffron

Pinch of kosher salt

Fresh fruit or fruit compote, if desired, for serving

1. Make the crust: Sift the powdered sugar into a medium bowl. Add the cubed butter, then use a hand mixer to beat until smooth. Beat in 3 of the egg yolks until they are incorporated. Sift the flour into the bowl and stir until the mixture forms a loose, crumbly dough. If the dough is too dry to come together when pinched, mix in another egg yolk.

2. Form the dough into a ball and put it between 2 sheets of parchment paper. Using a rolling pin, flatten the dough into an 11-inch (28 cm) disk that's ⅛ to ¼ inch thick. Put the dough and parchment in the refrigerator to chill for 20 minutes. Lightly grease a 9-inch (1 inch deep) tart pan with butter and set aside.

3. Once the dough has chilled for 20 minutes, remove it from the refrigerator and discard the parchment. Transfer the dough to the prepared tart pan and gently press it into the bottom and up the sides. Cover the pan in plastic wrap or foil and return it to the refrigerator for 20 minutes more.

4. Preheat the oven to 375°F/190°C. Set the oven rack in the lower middle of the oven.

5. Once the pan is chilled, remove it from the refrigerator. Trim any excess dough hanging over the edge of the pan, then use a fork to prick the bottom of the crust all over. Line the crust with parchment and fill with pie weights. Put it on a rimmed baking sheet on the lower-middle rack of the oven until the edges begin to brown, about 12 minutes. Remove from the oven and carefully remove the parchment and pie weights. To prevent the top edge of the crust from browning too much, cover with a pie shield or aluminum foil. Return the empty crust to the oven for 10 minutes, or until the base is lightly browned all over. Remove from the oven and allow to cool on a wire rack for about 10 minutes.

6. Reduce the oven temperature to 350°F/180°C. Set the oven rack in the middle of the oven.

continues

Tart de Bry

continued

7. Make the filling: Remove and discard the rind from the Brie. Cut the Brie into small pieces and add them to a food processor with the 6 beaten egg yolks. Blend until smooth. Add the ginger, sugar, saffron, and salt and blend to combine.

8. Spoon the cheese mixture into the cooled tart crust and smooth the top. Bake the tart on the middle rack of the oven until the top is set and begins to brown, 30 to 40 minutes. Remove the tart from the oven and allow it to cool for 10 minutes before serving. This is best served with fresh fruit or fruit compote, if desired.

Cook's Notes: The medieval crust would likely have been made of flour and lard and was not often meant to be eaten but simply used as a serving vessel. Since this version of the recipe is meant to be eaten as a modern tart, I have opted for a richer crust.

For a stronger flavor of Brie, keep some of the rind and sprinkle chopped pieces of it on the cooled tart crust before adding the filling.

Hippocras

City/Region: England
Time Period: c. 1390

Making hippocras with
a Hippocratic Sleeve

The first recipes for spiced wine in Europe come from the Ancient Roman cookbook by Apicius *De re coquinaria* and the practice of spiking wine with spice was one of the few things to survive the fall of Rome. Throughout Spain a drink called piment is found in the recipe collections of the Early Middle Ages, and in the 1180s Chrétien de Troyes wrote an Arthurian legend where Sir Perceval ends each meal with a cup of the piment before continuing his search for the Holy Grail. Soon the term "piment" was replaced by "hippocras" or "ypocras," derived from the *manicum hippocraticum*, or Hippocratic Sleeve, through which the spices are strained. Don't worry if you can't find a Hippocratic Sleeve to make this recipe, as a jelly bag makes an excellent stand-in.

Hippocras was thought to help indigestion after large meals and, more important, could balance the humors. The theory of the four humors guided medicine for centuries and the medieval mind was obsessed with keeping their blood, yellow bile, black bile, and phlegm in balance. Food was the preferred method of doing this, as daily bloodlettings can get tedious. Each food was assigned some degree of hot or cold and wet or dry, so the best way to offset a glass of cold, wet wine was with some hot, dry spices. And if Geoffrey Chaucer is to be believed, and he often is, hippocras was an excellent way to rev up the medieval libido:

> *He drinketh hippocras, claree, and vernage*
> *Of spices hot to increase his courage.*
> —Chaucer, "The Merchant's Tale"

continues

Hippocras

continued

In Spain, hippocras was often made with sugar, fresh herbs, and pieces of fruit and eventually evolved into sangria. In Northern Europe, the spiced drink was consigned to the cold winter months and the holiday season. Mulled wine and wassail punch are still must-haves in England at Christmas, and every *Weihnachtsmarkt* in Germany will gladly serve you a boot of glühwein.

In Sweden and the Nordic countries, they've kept the spiced wine tradition alive with glogg, though it's often given a splash of rum or whiskey to help bring the drinker an extra bit of good cheer. While our medieval hippocras recipe doesn't have any hard liquor, I wouldn't fault you for taking a page from the Swedes if the spirit moves you.

MAKES 10 SERVINGS   **COOK TIME:** 2 DAYS

2 (750 ml) bottles semisweet white or light red wine

5 sticks of cinnamon

3 tablespoons dried ginger pieces or 1 tablespoon ground ginger

1 teaspoon chopped dried galangal root (see page 12)

1 teaspoon ground cloves

1 teaspoon ground long pepper (see page 13)

1 teaspoon ground nutmeg

1 teaspoon dried marjoram

1 teaspoon ground cardamom

½ teaspoon ground grains of paradise (see page 12)

½ teaspoon ground cinnamon

¼ teaspoon dried spikenard root (see page 13)

1. Pour the wine into a large pitcher. Add the cinnamon sticks, ginger, galangal, cloves, pepper, nutmeg, marjoram, cardamom, grains of paradise, ground cinnamon, and spikenard and stir well. Cover the container with a cloth and set in a cool, dark space for 2 days. Gently stir the hippocras three times a day.

2. After 2 days, position a jelly bag in a second pitcher and set a strainer over the jelly bag. Slowly pour the hippocras through the strainer into the jelly bag and allow to slowly drain into the second pitcher. Do this gradually, as the dregs will build up in the jelly bag and may need to be scooped out to allow the hippocras to continue straining. The spices can be reused as a base for a second pitcher of hippocras.

3. The hippocras can be served cold, at room temperature, or hot.

Dillegrout or Bardolf

City/Region: England
Time Period: c. 1425

FROM HISTORY

Take almond milk, and draw it up thick with vernage, and let it boil, and meat of capons boiled, and put thereto; and cast thereto sugar, cloves, mace, pine nuts, and ginger, minced; and take chickens parboiled, and chopped, and pull off the skin, and boil all together, and in the setting down from the fire, put thereto a little vinegar mixed with powder of ginger, and a little water or rose, and make the potage hanginge, and serve it forth.

—Arundel Manuscript 334

Matilda of Flanders

It's rare that we know a specific decade or even century that a certain dish was first served, but when it comes to dillegrout, we likely know the exact day it was first presented. It's gone by many names over the centuries, including dillegrout, Bardolf, girunt, and malpigernoun to name a few, but regardless of the name, it was first presented to Matilda of Flanders, the Queen of England, wife of William the Conqueror, at her coronation banquet on May 11, 1068. The Conqueror's cook, Tezelin, prepared the dish for the royal couple, and it was decreed that it should be made for every coronation thenceforth.

The preparation of dillegrout was linked not with the royal cook, but with his home. The king gave Tezelin the manor of Addington as a serjeanty to be passed down the generations, and at every royal coronation from 1068 to 1821 whoever held the manor of Addington was required to prepare three bowls of the sweetly spiced stew: one for the monarch, one for the Archbishop of Canterbury, and another for whomever else the king or queen deemed deserving. Since the name of the dish keeps changing throughout history, its link to Addington is the only way we have any idea what the dish was like. The only surviving recipe, the one used in this book, calls the dish Bardolf, likely named after the lord of Addington during the reign of Richard II:

continues

Dillegrout
or Bardolf

continued

The lord of the manor [Baron William Bardolf] in Addington, Surrey . . . is said to have held Addington by the serve of finding a cook to dress such victuals in the King's kitchen . . . on the day of his coronation, or of finding a person who should make for him a certain pottage called the mess of Gyron; or if fat is added to it, is called Maupygernon.
— Thomas Blount, *Tenures of Land & Customs of Manors*

As the centuries moved on and cuisine evolved, the medieval dillegrout did not and it lost favor with the royal palate. In 1661, Charles II accepted the dish as custom dictated but then did not eat it, and on July 19, 1821, it made a final appearance at the coronation of George IV, unable to make the leap to the Victorian age.

MAKES 6 SERVINGS   **COOK TIME:** 3 HOURS 15 MINUTES

1 cup (120 g) blanched almond slivers

3 cups (710 ml) sweet white wine (such as a sweet Riesling or Moscato)

1½ pounds (.6 kg) skinless chicken breast

1½ pounds (.6 kg) skinless capon or chicken thighs

¼ cup (50 g) dark brown sugar

⅛ teaspoon ground clove

½ teaspoon ground mace

¼ cup (35 g) pine nuts

½ teaspoon dried chopped ginger or ground ginger

1 teaspoon sea salt

⅛ cup (30 ml) white wine vinegar

1 teaspoon (5 ml) rosewater

½ teaspoon ground ginger

1. Soak the almonds in cool water for 2 hours, then drain them. Add them to a blender with the sweet white wine and blend until the almonds are fully ground. Place a fine-mesh strainer in a bowl and line it with a nut milk bag or cheesecloth. Pour the almond and wine mixture through the cloth and allow it to drain until no more liquid comes through the cloth. Then gently squeeze the bag to remove any remaining liquid, allowing the strainer to catch any particles of almond. Discard the ground almond and set the bowl of almond milk aside.

2. Bring a pot of water to a boil on the stove and place the whole chicken breast in, parboiling for 10 minutes. Then remove and chop the chicken breast into bite-size pieces and set aside.

3. Chop the capon or chicken thighs into small pieces and then pound them until it becomes a pulp, then add to a pot and cover with the almond milk. Set the pot over high heat and bring to a boil. Once it is boiling, add the sugar, clove, mace, pine nuts, dried ginger, salt, and chicken breast (this should not be pounded) to the pot and reduce the heat to medium low. Then cover the pot and let it simmer for 1 hour, stirring occasionally to prevent burning the bottom of the pot.

4. Once the dillegrout has simmered for an hour, mix in the white wine vinegar, rosewater, and ground ginger and simmer, uncovered, for another 5 minutes. Then remove it from the heat and serve it forth.

King Hardikanute, 'midst Danes and Saxons stout,
Caroused on nut-brown ale, and dined on grout;
Which dish its pristine honour still maintains,
And when each king is crowned, in splendour reigns.
—*The Art of Cookery* by Dr. William King

The Third and Last Challenge by the Champion during King George IV's Coronation Banquet in Westminster Hall by Denis Dighton

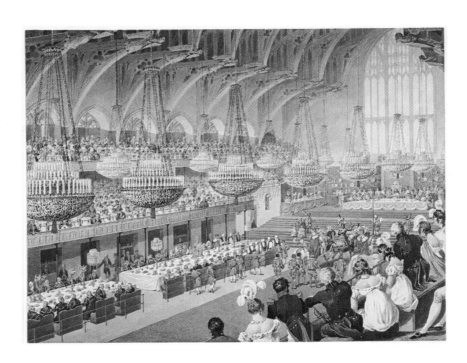

Crustade Lombarde

City/Region: England
Time Period: c. 1450

Crustade Lombarde is a rich dessert fit for a king or, at times, a monk. While we usually think of the ideal medieval monk as a man who spent the day at prayer or else toiling in the garden, subsisting on meager meals of bland food, that was not always the case. True, Saint Benedict prescribed: "Above all things . . . over-indulgence must be avoided and a monk must never be overtaken by indigestion" (*St. Benedict's Rule for Monasteries*).[1] But many a monk, living on the wealth of the monasteries, enjoyed a more gluttonous lifestyle. It was written of the twelfth-century Abbot Samson of Bury St. Edmunds: "Sweet milk, honey, and such like similar sweet things, he ate with greater appetite than other food" (*The Chronicle of Jocelin of Brakelond*).

When the twelfth-century chronicler and Archdeacon of Brecon, Gerald of Wales, traveled to the abbey at Canterbury, he expected to see the ascetic *Rule of St. Benedict* being followed to the letter, but when he sat down to a meal there were a vast number of dishes with sauces and spices as well as cups flowing with mead and every sort of wine he could think of.

A large meal became so necessary to the monks of St. Swithin in Winchester that Gerald tells of what happened when their bishop cut three dishes from their meal. They took their case all the way up to Henry II, throwing themselves down into the mud, crying and begging him to restore their dinner, but when the king was told that they still had ten dishes at their table, he scolded them as he, as king, only had three.

And so to find a dish worthy of a monk's table, I've decided the sweet and custardy dessert known as Crustade Lombarde, or Lombardy Custard, would fit the bill.

MAKES ONE 9-INCH TART   **COOK TIME:** 1 HOUR 45 MINUTES

FOR THE CRUST:
½ cup (65 g) powdered sugar

½ cup (115 g) salted butter, chilled but pliable and cut into ½-inch cubes

3 or 4 large egg yolks

1¾ cups (240 g) all-purpose flour

FOR THE FILLING:
15 pitted dates, chopped into ½-inch pieces

15 prunes, chopped into ½-inch pieces

¼ cup (30 g) finely chopped bone marrow

1 cup (235 ml) heavy whipping cream

2 large eggs

3 tablespoons minced parsley

1 teaspoon kosher salt

¼ cup (50 g) granulated sugar

1. Make the crust: Sift the powdered sugar into a large bowl and add the cubed butter. Beat until smooth. Beat in 3 egg yolks one at a time. Sift in the flour and mix until it has just formed a loose, crumbly dough. If the dough is too crumbly to come together, add another egg yolk. Form the dough into a ball and place it between 2 sheets of parchment. Roll into an 11-inch (28 cm) disk, ⅛ to ¼ inch thick. Chill the dough in the parchment in the refrigerator for 20 minutes. Using butter or nonstick cooking spray, lightly grease a 9-inch tart tin.

2. Once the dough has chilled, remove it from the refrigerator and discard the parchment. Transfer the dough to the prepared pie tin, folding the rim of the dough under itself and crimping along the edge. Cover the tin in plastic wrap or foil and return to the refrigerator for 20 minutes.

3. Preheat the oven to 375°F/190°C.

4. Remove the tin from the refrigerator and discard the plastic wrap. Use a fork to prick the bottom of the crust all over, then line it with aluminum foil and fill with pie weights. Set it on a baking sheet and bake on the lower-middle rack for 15 minutes or until the edges begin to brown. Then remove it from the oven and reduce the temperature to 350°F/175°C.

5. While the crust is still hot, remove the pie weights and foil, and sprinkle the bottom of the crust with the chopped dates, prunes, and marrow. Return it to the oven for 10 minutes. If the edge of the crust begins to darken too much, set a pie shield around the rim of

continues

Crustade
Lombarde

continued

the tin. Once the crust is baked, remove it and let it cool completely on a wire rack while you prepare the filling.

6. Make the filling: Combine the cream and eggs in a large bowl and whisk until soft peaks form. Add parsley and salt and whisk until just incorporated. Pour the cream and egg mixture into the cooled crust. Smooth the top and sprinkle sugar all over the top. If the exposed crust is fully baked, cover with a pie shield. Return it to the oven and bake for 20 minutes or until the filling sets and the top starts to brown. There should still be a slight wobble in the middle. Remove and set on a wire rack to cool before serving.

History Fact: The idea of the corpulent monk had become so standard that by the fourteenth century Chaucer described the monk in *The Canterbury Tales* by saying: "He was a lord ful fat and in good poynt."

Farts of Portingale

✕✕✕✕✕✕✕✕✕✕✕✕✕✕✕✕

City/Region: England
Time Period: 1597

Sixteenth-century kitchen
with cook and maid

The year was 1504, and the Right Honourable William Warham was enthroned as the new Archbishop of Canterbury. After the ceremony there was a grand feast with only the most noble and regal guests of England in attendance. But, despite the pomp and circumstance and general hoity-toityness of it all, we have to allow that at some point in the evening it is possible that the new archbishop uttered the phrase "what a delectable fart." Oh yes, Farts of Portingale made it onto the menu.

I wish I could tell you that the name of these balls of meat or dough was the casualty of an etymological twist of fate, but in reality, it seems that the name is just a crude joke. In the fifteenth century, Germany and Austria had a dish called *Nonnenfürtze*, or nun farts, and the seventeenth-century French cookbook *Le cuisiner françois* includes a sugared beignet called *pets du putain*, or farts of a whore. These continental farts were all pastry and one recipe was for Farts of Portingale (an early English spelling of "Portugal") that were also closer to a donut hole than a meatball and whose name may have come about due to their being puffed up with hot air; our ancestors were juvenile if nothing else. But the name stuck and became applied to other small, round foods such as the farts that Thomas Dawson describes in his recipe.

⅓ cup (60 g) dried currants
(see page 12)

1 teaspoon kosher salt

½ teaspoon ground mace

¼ teaspoon freshly ground black
pepper

⅛ teaspoon ground clove

1 pound (450 g) trimmed mutton
or lamb, minced very small in a
food processor

⅓ cup (60 g) pitted dates, minced
to the size of currants

1 quart (1 liter) unsalted beef
broth

Gravy or mild raspberry sauce,
if desired, for serving

1. Soak the currants in water for 1 hour, then drain.

2. In a small bowl, stir together the salt, mace, black pepper, and clove. Sprinkle it over the minced lamb in a medium bowl and toss the mixture with your hands until the spice is incorporated. Add the minced dates and currants and mix until well dispersed. Divide the mixture into 12 to 15 tightly formed balls slightly smaller than a golf ball.

3. Pour the beef broth into a medium saucepan over medium heat and bring to a gentle boil. If using a larger pot, add another quart of broth to ensure that it is deep enough to cover the balls. Once boiling, carefully set the balls, four at a time, into the beef broth and boil until they reach an internal temperature of 145°F/63°C, for 6 to 7 minutes.

4. Using a slotted spoon, remove the balls and set on a wire rack to drain. Repeat until all the farts have been cooked. Serve warm. These are excellent with a gravy or mild raspberry sauce, if desired.

Cook's Note: The word "currant" comes from the Ancient Greek city of Corinth. But they were not currants, the soft berries that grow on bushes, but dried grapes. Raisins of Corinth (often called Zante currants today) were the original currants, though other dried currants, including those from the bushes, have been used in baking for centuries.

Soul Cakes

City/Region: England
Time Period: c. 1600

FROM HISTORY

Take flower & sugar & nutmeg & cloves & mace
& sweet butter & sack & a little ale barm, beat
your spice & put in your butter & your sack,
cold, then work it well all together & make it in
little cakes & so bake them, if you will you may
put in some saffron into them or fruit.

—*Elinor Fettiplace's Receipt Book*[1]

Nobody knows when the tradition of soul cakes began, but some trace it all the way back to the Celtic festival of Samhain, pronounced "SAH-win," when it's said the inhabitants of the British Isles would serve small cakes to appease the Aos Sí, mischievous spirits and fairies that cross into our world during the harvest festival to wreak havoc. But it's not until the Middle Ages, long after Christianity had taken hold in the isles, that we see real evidence for something called soul cakes.

On All Hallows' Day, celebrated November 1, and the evening before, All Hallows' Eve, later Halloween, adults and children alike would go door to door "souling," offering songs and prayers for the departed loved ones of their neighbors.

And this service came at the cheap price of a cup of ale or else a sweet cake known as a soul cake, often decorated with a cross on top. The practice spread throughout Britain, merging with other traditions. In Wales the cakes were less of a gift for prayers and more of a bribe to keep Death itself away from the door. When the knocker would ask for a cake, they would follow the request with a threat to encourage Death to harm those on the other side of the door should cakes not be given, a harsh precursor to the more innocuous trick-or-treat of today.

In parts of England, those going souling would carry candles or lanterns as they went around to light their way and ward off witches and demons. They would often dress as the very evil spirits they were trying to frighten or else their favorite saint. For example, a costume based on Saint Ceolfrith

continues

Soul Cakes

continued

of Monkwearmouth, contributor to the Codex Amiatinus Bible, might seem odd for a child begging for a Snickers or Baby Ruth today, but in the thirteenth century, it would be as normal as a *Ghostbusters* costume. Odder would be if, instead of a candy bar, you gave the trick-or-treater one of these wonderful, but mildly sweet to our modern palate, soul cakes, so best to keep them for family and friends.

MAKES 12 CAKES   **COOK TIME:** 4 HOURS 40 MINUTES

¾ cup (90 g) dried currants (see page 12), or other diced dried fruit

¾ cup (180 ml) sweet sherry

6 to 8 saffron threads

½ cup (120 ml) dark ale

6 tablespoons (85 g) unsalted butter, melted

4 cups (480 g) all-purpose flour

2¼ teaspoons (7 g) instant dry yeast

½ cup (100 g) granulated sugar

1½ teaspoons kosher salt

½ teaspoon ground nutmeg

½ teaspoon ground mace

¼ teaspoon ground clove

1 large egg plus 1 tablespoon water, for egg wash

1. Soak the currants in a bowl of warm water for 30 minutes. Drain, pat dry, and set aside.

2. Mix the sherry with the saffron in a small bowl and set aside for 30 minutes.

3. Mix the ale, sherry with saffron, and melted butter in a medium bowl. In a large bowl, whisk together the flour, yeast, sugar, salt, nutmeg, mace, and clove. Add the ale, sherry, and butter mixture to the flour and mix to combine. The dough should be sticky but workable. If it is too sticky, add more flour, 1 tablespoon at a time. Add half of the currants, reserving the other half for decoration, and mix to incorporate evenly, then knead until the gluten is fully developed. Once the dough is kneaded, set it in a bowl and cover. Allow to rise until it has doubled in size, 2 to 2½ hours.

4. Once it has risen, punch down the dough and divide into twelve pieces. Form each piece into a cake by rolling the dough into a ball as you would for a dinner roll and then gently pressing it down to flatten it. Set the cakes onto two lined baking sheets, 2 inches apart, and cover loosely with plastic. Allow to rise for 1 hour.

5. Preheat the oven to 350°F/175°C.

6. After the formed cakes are risen, whisk the egg and water together in a small bowl, then brush the egg wash onto the cakes. Add the remaining currants as decoration. Bake for 20 to 25 minutes or until the top is golden brown. Remove from the oven and place on a wire rack to cool.

Pancakes

✕✕✕✕✕✕✕✕✕✕✕✕✕✕✕

City/Region: England
Time Period: 1658

The Fight Between Carnival and Lent by Pieter Bruegel the Elder

> ## FROM HISTORY
>
> *To make fine Pan-cakes fryed without Butter or Lard. Take a pint of Cream, and six new laid Egs, beat them very well together, put in a quarter of a pound of Sugar, and one nutmeg or a little beaten Mace (which you please) and so much flower as will thicken almost as much as ordinarily Pan-cake batter; your Pan must be heated reasonably hot & wiped with a clean Cloth, this done put in your Batter as thick or thin as you please.*
>
> —W. M., *The Compleat Cook*

Pancakes come in all shapes and sizes and are made with all sorts of ingredients. From the einkorn pancake that Ötzi the Iceman made fifty-three hundred years ago before he was frozen for posterity, to the savory *okonomiyaki* of Japan, which might include octopus or cabbage. But these seventeenth-century English pancakes are closer to what one might find at IHOP, albeit with more nutmeg. These are the pancakes of Shrove Tuesday.

Shrove Tuesday is the day before Ash Wednesday, which ushers in the forty-day fast of Lent. While many people who observe Lent today give up chocolate or alcohol, the population of medieval and Renaissance England gave up much more, making Shrove Tuesday their last chance to gorge themselves into a pancake stupor.

> *On the morning of Shrove Tuesday the whole kingdom is quiet, but by that time that the clock strikes eleven, there is a bell rung, called the Pancake-bell, the sound whereof makes thousands of people distracted, and forgetful of manners or of humanity; then there is a thing called wheaten flour, which the sulphury, Necromantic cooks do mingle with water, eggs, spice and other tragical, magical enchantments, then they put*

continues

Pancakes

continued

*it by little and little into a frying-pan of boiling suet, where
it makes a confused, dismal hissing (like the Lernean snakes
in the reeds of Acheron, Styx or Phlegeton) until at last, by
the skill of the cooks it is transformed into the form of . . .
a Pancake, which ominous incantation the ignorant people do
devour very greedily.*
—John Taylor, *Jack a Lent*

Sated on pancakes, the people spent the rest of the day playing games and sports, the most popular being a perilous pastime known as "mob football." Then, bellies full and bodies bruised, they staggered to church to be shriven, that is, to have a priest hear their confession and absolve them of all they'd done that day and in the previous year. Still today, in villages all around England, Shrove Tuesday is celebrated with pancakes, games, and an afternoon in church.

MAKES 12 TO 15 LARGE PANCAKES **COOK TIME:** 37 MINUTES

6 large eggs

1 pint (475 ml) heavy whipping cream

½ cup (113 g) dark brown sugar

2 teaspoons ground nutmeg or 1 teaspoon ground mace

2 cups (240 g) all-purpose flour

1 or 2 teaspoons unsalted butter or cooking spray

1. Whisk the eggs in a large bowl until frothy. Add the cream and whisk until smooth. Add the sugar and nutmeg or mace and whisk to combine. Fold in the flour until just combined, with no flecks of flour remaining. Cover the bowl and allow the batter to rest in the refrigerator for 30 minutes.

2. Heat a griddle or large skillet over medium-low heat. Melt 1 or 2 teaspoons butter, just enough to coat the griddle or skillet, or coat with cooking spray. Once the butter is melted and no longer foaming, ladle the batter onto the griddle or skillet. These are meant to be large pancakes made one at a time, but they can be made smaller. The first pancake may require a slightly higher heat. Cook the pancake until the batter loses its shine, all of the bubbles on top have popped, and the bottom is a golden brown, 2 to 4 minutes. Then flip the pancake and cook until golden brown, about 2 minutes. Add more butter to the griddle or skillet as needed.

Pumpion Pie

City/Region: England
Time Period: 1670

FROM HISTORY

*To make a Pumpion Pie—Take a Pumpion,
pare it, and cut it in thin slices, dip it in
beaten Eggs and Herbs shred small, and fry
it till it be enough, then lay it into a Pie with
Butter, Raisins, Currans, Sugar and Sack,
and in the bottom some sharp Apples; when
it is baked, butter it and serve it in.*

—Hannah Woolley, *The Queene-like Closet; or, Rich Cabinet*

Early pumpkin pies were very different from the creamy custard pies we enjoy today. Some were closer to a pumpkin cheesecake, such as a recipe found in Bartolomeo Scappi's *Opera dell'arte cucinare* (see recipe for Torta d'Herbe Communi, page 133), and some were crustless, being baked in the actual pumpkin itself. This recipe, for Pumpion Pie, from *The Queene-like Closet; or, Rich Cabinet* by Hannah Woolley reflects just how new the ingredient was to Europe; they hadn't even added a *k* to the spelling yet. While it includes a crust and is nothing like a cheesecake, it does have some flavors that might seem strange if found in a dessert on your Thanksgiving table today.

Pumpkin pie has long been associated with this most American of holidays, though it was most certainly not served at the very first Thanksgiving in 1621. When the Pilgrims and Wampanoag sat down to share an autumn harvest feast, they did so with no flour for crusts, no sugar for filling, and no ovens for baking. Instead, if they enjoyed pumpkins at all, they were likely roasted over an open fire. But even though the gourd may not have started out in pie form, by the late eighteenth century pumpkin pie was a staple of the New England Thanksgiving dinner. In the 1827 novel *Northwood* by Sarah Josepha Buell Hale she describes the feast:

> *There was a huge plumb pudding, custards, and pies of every
> name and description ever known in Yankee land; yet the
> pumpkin pie occupied the most distinguished niche.*

continues

Pumpion Pie

continued

Yet distinguished niche or no, both the dessert and the holiday had trouble expanding beyond New England to the rest of the United States. For seventeen years, Hale, an abolitionist as well as author, petitioned US presidents to adopt Thanksgiving as a national holiday. As it was seen as a Yankee holiday, the southern states were vehemently against it, opting instead for state holidays and sweet potato pie. Not until 1863, with the Civil War raging, did Abraham Lincoln grant Ms. Hale's petitions when he established the last Thursday of November as a national day of Thanksgiving. (It didn't become the fourth Thursday in November until 1941.) The holiday and the pie have remained popular ever since.

MAKES ONE 9-INCH PIE   **COOK TIME:** 1 HOUR 40 MINUTES

1 small sugar or pie pumpkin

2 apples (tart varieties, such as Granny Smith)

3 tablespoons chopped fresh rosemary

3 tablespoons chopped fresh parsley

2 tablespoons chopped fresh thyme

3 large eggs, beaten

Lard or vegetable oil, for frying

4 tablespoons (57 g) salted butter, softened

⅓ cup (50 g) dark raisins

⅓ cup (50 g) currants

½ cup (100 g) granulated sugar

¼ cup (60 ml) cream sherry

1 (9-inch) piecrust

History Fact: The first pumpkin custard pie recipe, like those we eat today, appeared in Amelia Simmons's *American Cookery* in 1796.

1. Preheat oven to 425°F/220°C.

2. Cut off the top stem of the pumpkin, then cut the pumpkin in half. Remove the peel from each half of the pumpkin and scoop out the seeds. Slice the pumpkin into thin slices, about ⅛ inch thick, then set aside. Peel and core the apples and slice into thin slices about ⅛ inch thick.

3. Mix the rosemary, parsley, and thyme with the beaten eggs in a medium bowl. Dip the pumpkin slices into the mixture, to coat. Coat the bottom of a large skillet with ¼ inch oil and set over medium heat. Once the oil is hot, working in batches, place a single layer of pumpkin slices on the bottom and fry until soft, turning once, 5 to 7 minutes. Set the fried pumpkin on a wire rack to drain any excess oil. Discard any bits of egg coating that remain in the pan. Repeat until all of the pumpkin is fried, adding more oil if necessary.

4. Transfer the fried pumpkin to a large bowl. Mix in 2 tablespoons of the butter, raisins, currants, sugar, and sherry. Line the bottom of the piecrust with the apple slices, pour the pumpkin mixture over the apples, and smooth the top.

5. Bake for 20 minutes, then reduce heat to 375°F/190°C and bake 40 to 50 minutes longer, or until the top of the pie is bubbling. If the crust begins to darken too much, cover with a pie shield or aluminum foil. Once the pie is baked, remove it from the oven and set a on a wire rack. While the pie is still hot, scatter the 2 remaining tablespoons of butter on the top of the pie and allow it to melt into the crust. Cool completely before slicing.

Everlasting Syllabub

✕✕✕✕✕✕✕✕✕✕✕✕✕✕✕

City/Region: England
Time Period: 1747

FROM HISTORY

To Make Everlasting Syllabub Take five half pints of thick Cream, and half a Pint of Sack, the Juice of two Seville Oranges, or Lemons, grate in just the yellow Rind of three Lemons, and a Pound of double-refined Sugar well beat, and sifted. Mix all together with a Spoonful of Orange-flower Water, beat it well together with a Whisk half an Hour, then with a Spoon fill your Glasses.

—*The Art of Cookery Made Plain and Easy* by Hannah Glasse

Samuel Pepys by
John Hayls

The wonderfully named syllabub began life as a drink made by curdling cream with wine or cider, then letting the curdled cream float on top while the drinker sipped the liquor beneath. Some considered it a drink for ladies only, but by the seventeenth century it was enjoyed by all manner of polite society. Samuel Pepys wrote in his diary of going to Commissioner Pett's house after church, where Pepys "had a syllabub, and saw his closet, which come short of what I expected, but there was fine modells of ships in it indeed, whose worth I could not judge of."

By the eighteenth century, the float of curdled cream evolved into the bulk of the drink and eventually we find recipes for Everlasting Syllabub, which lower the level of liquor and include a lot more cream, sugar, and whipping to produce a boozy, often flavored, whipped cream that can be eaten alone or, as Hannah Glasse suggests, appear as a layer in a trifle. The excessive whipping (Hannah prescribes a half hour) made this Everlasting Syllabub less appealing to the casual imbiber of foamy wine drinks, until a Dr. Stephen Hales devised an engine with a tube, on one end of which he affixed a tin box with holes and on the other a pair of bellows, allowing one to "blow up cream into syllabub with great expedition" (*Old English Glasses* by Albert Hartshorne [1897]).

But if you are without a syllabub engine in your kitchen, feel free to use an electric mixer.

continues

Everlasting Syllabub

continued

The Art of Cookery Made Plain and Easy frontispiece

MAKES 12 TO 15 SERVINGS   **COOK TIME:** 10 MINUTES

2½ cups (590 ml) heavy whipping cream (or double cream)

1¾ cups (225 g) confectioners' sugar

½ cup (120 ml) of a sweet wine (white port or sherry)

¼ cup (60 ml) Seville orange juice (if you cannot find a Seville orange, use half of a lemon and half of a sweet orange)

Grated zest of 2 lemons

1 teaspoon orange blossom water

Orange or lemon twist, if desired, to garnish

1. Pour the cream into a large bowl and slowly add the sugar, whisking continuously until the sugar is dissolved. While continuing to whisk, add in the wine, orange juice, lemon zest, and orange blossom water. Whisk in a stand mixer or with a handheld mixer on medium until stiff enough not to splash out of the bowl. Mix on high speed until the mixture forms stiff peaks, 5 to 7 minutes.

2. Serve with a garnish of orange or lemon twist, if desired. Can be refrigerated for up to 3 days.

History Fact: In 1669, Sir Kenelm Digby provided a recipe for a nonalcoholic syllabub using a plum syrup.

Parmesan Cheese Ice Cream

City/Region: England
Time Period: 1789

> ## FROM HISTORY
>
> *No. 150. Parmasan Cheese Ice Cream—Take six eggs, half a pint of syrup and a pint of cream; put them into a stewpan and boil them until it begins to thicken; then rasp three ounces of parmasan cheese, mix and pass them through a sieve, and freeze it.*
>
> —Frederick Nutt, *The Complete Confectioner*

Hero's recruiting at Kelsey's; - or - Guard-Day at St. James's by James Gillray

Iced desserts date back thousands of years. The Greeks and Romans sweetened mountain snow with honey and wine, and during the Tang Dynasty (AD 618 to 906) in China, fermented milk heated with camphor was cooled and poured over ice. By the eleventh century, the Persians were making sharbat, later called sherbet by Sir Thomas Herbert following his travels in the 1620s:

> *Their liquor is sometimes fair water, sugar, rose-water, and juice of lemons mixed, and sugar confected with citrons, violets or other sweet flowers; and for the more delicacy, sometimes a mixture of amber; this we call sherbet.*

But something akin to modern ice cream didn't appear until 1692, when Antonio Latini wrote a recipe for what he called "milk sorbet" flavored with lemon and pumpkin, then frozen with snow and salt. By the early 1700s, ice cream, or *crème glacée*, became all the rage in Paris and recipes begin to appear in cookbooks with standard ingredients like chocolate, coffee, and vanilla, along with some more interesting flavors like parmesan, avocado, asparagus, and foie gras. And while parmesan and foie gras ice cream never took off in the United States, Thomas Jefferson, after serving as ambassador to France in the 1780s, did return to Monticello with a handwritten recipe for French vanilla ice cream.

continues

Parmesan Cheese Ice Cream

continued

The dessert became wildly popular in the United States, though, being a labor-intensive treat, it remained available mostly to those with the time and money to churn it at home. Then, in 1843, Nancy Johnson of Philadelphia patented a mechanical hand-cranked ice cream–making machine that sped up the production for the home cook and paved the way for the commercial ice-cream industry. Not long after, every main street in America had an ice-cream parlor or soda shop where the town's kids would hang out. In the 1920s, as Prohibition set in, these hangouts for teens became a place for the entire family as the country's beer manufacturers, like Anheuser-Busch and Yuengling, switched to producing ice cream as a way to stay in business. By the 1930s, as beer and other liquor made a comeback, ice cream had found its way into the hearts of Americans, and it is now one of the most popular desserts in the world.

MAKES 1 QUART **COOK TIME:** 12 HOURS 40 MINUTES

5 large eggs at room temperature

2 cups (475 ml) heavy whipping cream

1 cup (235 ml) simple syrup, 1 to 1 ratio

3 ounces (85 g) Parmesan cheese, freshly grated

1. Allow all ingredients to come to room temperature before proceeding. Whisk eggs in a small saucepan until smooth. Add the cream and syrup and whisk to combine. Set the saucepan over medium-low heat and stir continuously with a whisk to prevent burning or clumping. The mixture will begin to thicken into a custard after 10 to 15 minutes. Remove it from the heat when it reaches 170°F (76°C). Another way to tell when it is thick enough is to dip a spoon in the custard and draw your finger across the back of the spoon. If a streak remains, then it is ready.

2. As soon as you remove the saucepan from the heat, add the Parmesan cheese and whisk continuously until fully melted into the custard. Pour the custard through a sieve into a clean bowl and let cool to room temperature or colder either in an ice bath or in the refrigerator.

3. Once the custard is cooled, pour it into an automatic or hand-cranked ice-cream maker and follow the instructions on the machine to freeze the custard into ice cream.

4. The ice cream will be soft and melt quickly, but to achieve a harder, longer-lasting scoop, place in the freezer for 12 hours before serving.

Sally Lunn Buns

City/Region: England
Time Period: 1826

FROM HISTORY

Make them as French bread, but dissolve some sugar in the hot milk. Mould into the form of cakes. A little saffron boiled in the milk enriches the colour of these or any other cakes.

—Margaret Dods, *The Cook and Housewife's Manual*

The Sally Lunn Bakery is one of my favorite stops to make when I visit the ancient city of Bath, England. As there is always a line around the block, I'm always in good company, and when you taste the sweet, pillowy goodness of a Sally Lunn Bun you'll understand why.

The origin of the bun and the real Sally Lunn is up for debate, but those at the bakery will tell you that in the late 1680s a young Huguenot woman named Solange Luyon fled from France, where she had been persecuted for her Protestant faith. Upon her arrival in Bath, she found work at a bakery in Lilliput Alley, where she sold the baker's wares on the street. In the evenings, when the medieval oven was not in use, she would bake the brioche-like buns that she'd known back home in France. One day, her employer tasted one, fell in love with it, and began selling it upstairs, giving full credit to his employee, Solange Luyon. The English customers stumbled over the name and eventually anglicized it to Sally Lunn. Is this romantic story true? Doubtful. But what's not doubtful is that by the late eighteenth century the bun had become the toast (also wonderful un-toasted) of Bath just as the city was becoming the place to be seen for England's high society.

Georgian Bath featured the Public Breakfast, a chance to mingle with the elite in the Pleasure Gardens and to sip Bath's healing waters and enjoy a Sally Lunn. But in 1780, the author Philip Thicknesse offered a warning against this practice in *The Valetudinarians Bath Guide*. He says that many of the visitors "first drink three pints or a quart of the Bath waters, and then sit down to a meal of Sally Luns or hot spungy rolls . . . such a meal, few young men in full health can get over without feeling much inconvenience, and I have known and seen it produce almost instantaneous death to valetudinarians." But no need to worry about making this recipe, as I'm inclined to believe it to be the often-sulfurous waters of Bath rather than the buttery buns of Sally Lunn that might lead to one's demise.

MAKES 6 LARGE BUNS   **COOK TIME:** 3 HOURS

1¼ cups (280 ml) whole milk

¼ cup (50 g) sugar

6 tablespoons (85 g) unsalted butter at room temperature

2 or 3 saffron threads, optional, for color only

3¾ cups (450 g) bread flour

7 grams instant yeast

2 large eggs

Grated zest of 1 lemon

1½ teaspoons kosher salt

FOR THE EGG WASH:
1 large egg

1 tablespoon water

Butter, jam, or clotted cream, if desired, for serving

I. Warm the milk in a small saucepan over low heat. Do not let it boil. Once it is warm, add the sugar and whisk to dissolve. Then melt the butter in the mixture, stirring gently. If using saffron for color, add the threads to the milk and set mixture aside to cool to 110°F/43°C or cooler before adding it to the other ingredients.

2. Sift flour into a large bowl and whisk in the instant yeast. Once the milk mixture is cooled, pour it into the flour through a strainer to strain out the saffron threads, and mix until a ragged dough comes together. Add the eggs, lemon zest, and salt to the dough and mix until combined. Knead until you have a smooth dough. This is a very sticky dough and will not form into a ball. Set the dough in a bowl lightly greased with butter or vegetable oil, cover, and let rise for 60 to 90 minutes, or until doubled in size.

3. Once the dough has doubled, punch it down to remove any pockets of air and turn it out onto a lightly floured surface and separate into six pieces. Form dough into balls and place on lined baking sheet, slightly flattening into a cake. Cover and let rise for another 45 to 60 minutes.

4. Preheat the oven to 400°F/200°C.

5. Make the egg wash: Whisk the egg and water together until very smooth in a small bowl. Once the buns have risen, brush the tops with the egg wash and set them in the oven on the middle rack. Bake for 15 minutes or until golden, tenting them if they begin to darken too much. Once they are baked, cool on a wire rack and serve warm with butter, jam, or clotted cream, if desired.

History Fact: Another possible origin of the name comes from 1845, when Eliza Acton gives a recipe for a "rich French breakfast cake" called a Solimemne, derived from *soleil et lune*, meaning "sun and moon."

Christmas Pudding

✖✖✖✖✖✖✖✖✖✖✖✖✖

City/Region: England
Time Period: 1845

FROM HISTORY

To three ounces of flour, and the same weight of fine, lightly-grated bread-crumbs, add six of beef kidney-suet, chopped small, six of raisins weighed after they are stoned, six of well-cleaned currants, four ounces of minced apples, five of sugar, two of candied orange-rind, half a teaspoonful of nutmeg mixed with pounded mace, a very little salt, a small glass of brandy, and three whole eggs. Mix and beat these ingredients well together, tie them tightly in a thickly floured cloth, and boil them for three hours and a half. We can recommend this as a remarkably light small rich pudding: it may be served with German, wine, or punch sauce.

—Eliza Acton, *Modern Cookery for Private Families*

The Family Plum Pudding.

Whenever I take a bite of Christmas pudding, sometimes called plum pudding or figgy pudding, I intone those immortal words of Tiny Tim: "God bless us, every one." This usually gets old by the fourth or fifth bite, which is why I'm no longer allowed to bring Christmas pudding to my family's holiday dinner, but I digress. Sweet, fruit-filled boiled puddings have been a staple of the English holiday season for centuries. They became particularly popular when the English left their island to settle in places around the globe, because a boiled pudding makes a perfect long-distance gift. You can make it in June, then ship it to Canada, India, or Australia, because a journey of six months is but a blink in the life of a well-boiled pudding. An 1887 article in *Good Housekeeping* talks of a man named Colonel Hazard who received a pudding while he was gone on holiday and it sat for two years before he returned to eat it, after which he mused "that a good plum pudding, like the wheat found in the old Egyptian mummy cases, would keep all right for a thousand years."

These puddings followed soldiers across the seas so often that they became a symbol of the British Empire itself, often being depicted in political

Opposite: *The Family Plum Pudding* by Robert Seymour

Right: *The Plumb-pudding in danger - or - State Epicures taking un Petit Souper* by James Gillray

cartoons of the day. One called *The Plumb-pudding in danger* shows William Pitt and Napoleon Bonaparte carving up a pudding in the form of the globe, Britain receiving a noticeably larger slice.

In 1843, only two years before Ms. Acton wrote her recipe, Christmas pudding played a starring role in the most famous Christmas story ever, when Mrs. Cratchit prepared her family's holiday feast.

> *Hallo! A great deal of steam! The pudding was out of the copper. A smell like a washing-day! That was the cloth. A smell like an eating-house and a pastry-cook's next door to each other, with a laundress's next door to that! That was the pudding! In half a minute Mrs. Cratchit entered—flushed, but smiling proudly—with the pudding, like a speckled cannon-ball, so hard and firm, blazing in half of half-a-quartern of ignited brandy, and bedight with Christmas holly stuck into the top.*
> —Charles Dickens, *A Christmas Carol*

If your pudding turns out to look like a speckled cannonball, then you've done it correctly, but one thing to keep in mind is choosing when to make the pudding. Mrs. Cratchit was boiling hers on Christmas Day, but surely that was its second boiling, because a good pudding must age. In England, there is a specific day to make the pudding and it's over a month before Christmas.

continues

Christmas Pudding

continued

1 heaping cup (170 g) dark raisins

1 heaping cup (170 g) dried currants (see page 12)

1½ cups (170 g) shredded suet or frozen and grated butter/ shortening, plus more for cloth

⅔ cup (145 g) dark brown sugar

3 large eggs, beaten

⅓ cup (80 ml) brandy

¾ cup (90 g) all-purpose flour, plus more for cloth

¾ cup (85 g) dry bread crumbs

½ teaspoon ground nutmeg

¼ teaspoon ground mace

Pinch of kosher salt

1 small apple (120 g) peeled, cored, and finely chopped

¾ cup (60 g) candied orange peel

"Stir Up Sunday" is the last Sunday before the season of Advent, when we open calendars filled with old chocolate. It's the day that you stir up the ingredients for your pudding, though the name of the day comes not from the baking done that day, but a line from *The Book of Common Prayer* that would be heard in Anglican churches all over England that morning: "Stir up, we beseech thee, O Lord, the wills of thy faithful people." After that, everyone would head out of church for the kitchen to stir up their Christmas pudding.

MAKES 1 LARGE PUDDING (12 SERVINGS)
COOK TIME: 4 HOURS 30 MINUTES

1. This pudding can be made in a pudding basin and steamed, which is much easier, but here we are following Eliza Acton's instructions for boiling. You will need a large piece of calico or muslin at least 24 inches (60 cm) square, but preferably a little larger, as it will shrink. Do not use cheesecloth, as its weave is too loose. If the cloth has never been used to boil a pudding before, boil it in water for 20 minutes, then remove it from the heat and let it soak overnight. The next day, fill a large pot half-full of fresh water and boil the cloth again for 20 minutes. If the cloth has been used previously for puddings, only this second (20-minute) boiling is necessary.

2. While the cloth boils, soak the raisins and currants in warm water for 10 minutes, strain them, and then prepare the pudding.

3. Add the suet, brown sugar, eggs, and brandy to a large bowl and beat until smooth. In a separate bowl, whisk together the flour, bread crumbs, nutmeg, mace, and salt. Add the egg mixture to the dry ingredients and stir until just combined, then stir in the raisins, currants, apple, and candied orange peel until well incorporated. Set it aside as you finish preparing the pudding cloth.

4. Using tongs, remove the pudding cloth from the boiling water; leave the water boiling. Allow the cloth to cool to the point that you're able to handle it without burning yourself, or use rubber gloves. Lay the pudding cloth flat and rub a 16 x 16-inch (40 x 40 cm) square in the center of the cloth with a coating of suet/butter. Coat this with a heavy layer of flour, lightly pressing the flour down into the cloth. The goal is to make a watertight skin of butter and flour between the cloth and the pudding, so use more than you think is

A family sit around a table eating their Christmas meal and greet the arrival of the plum pudding which is being carried in on a large tray by Cecil Aldin

necessary, especially in the center. Once it's well floured, place the cloth, flour side up, in a medium bowl and spoon the pudding batter into the center of the cloth. While this can be done without putting it into a bowl, the curved sides will help keep the pudding shape as you form it into a ball. Once the pudding is shaped, gather up the ends of the cloth and twist to form a tight seal at the top of the pudding. Then take cooking string and tie it tightly around the cloth as close as possible to the pudding. Tie two ends of the cloth together to form a handle. Lift the pudding, give it one final shaping—we're aiming for a cannonball—and carefully lower it into the pot of boiling water. The water should come ¾ of the way up the sides of the pudding, no more. Cover the pot and boil for 4 hours. Every once in a while, check to make sure the water level hasn't dropped below halfway up the pudding. If it has, add more water that has already been boiled in a kettle; do not add water that is not already boiling.

5. Remove the pot from the heat and, using gloves, carefully remove the pudding from the pot and set it in a colander. Cut the string, untie the cloth, and peel it away from the pudding. Let it sit for 20 minutes before serving or place it in an airtight container in a cool place, or preferably the refrigerator, to age for up to 2 months. Every few days, pour a tablespoon of brandy over it to soak. When ready to serve, reboil the pudding, using the same floured-cloth technique, for 1 hour before serving.

Sea Biscuits (Hardtack)

✕◇✕◇✕◇✕◇✕◇✕◇✕◇✕◇✕

City/Region: England
Time Period: 1815

HMS Hercule by
Louis-Philippe Crépin

FROM HISTORY

Sea Biscuit is a sort of bread much dried, to make it keep for the use of the navy, and is good for a whole year after it is baked. The process of biscuit-baking for the navy is simple and ingenious, and is nearly as follows. A large lump of dough, consisting merely of flower and water, is mixed up together, and placed exactly in the centre of a raised platform, where a man sits upon a machine, called a horse, and literally rides up and down . . . till the dough is sufficiently kneaded. . . . One man . . . moulds the dough, till it has the appearance of muffins. [Another] stamps them on both sides with a mark. The business is to deposit in the oven seventy biscuits in a minute. . . . The biscuits thus baked are kept in repositories, which receive warmth from being placed in drying lofts over the ovens, till they are sufficiently dry to be packed into bags, without danger of getting mouldy.

—William Burney, *Falconer's A New Universal Dictionary of the Marine*

Sea biscuits, galettes, ship's biscuits, molar breakers, worm castles, hardtack. Many words referring to the same dry, dense, unfathomably hard piece of bread that has been the staple for military rations for centuries. All it is is flour and water, sometimes salt, baked until it has the consistency of a brick. As Benjamin Franklin said, "The ship biscuit is too hard for some sets of teeth." And I'd extend that to all sets of teeth, at least if you're set on keeping them. But no sailor would eat sea biscuits plain; rather, they'd be softened in water or beer or ground into crumbs and used to thicken stews with fun names like lobscouse, skilligalee, or Hell-Fired Stew.

continues

Sea Biscuits (Hardtack)

continued

While these biscuits found their way into the rations of soldiers up through World War I, they're most associated with the British navy of the seventeenth to nineteenth centuries. In the 1670s, the English diarist Samuel Pepys moonlit as a naval official in charge of victuals for the King's Navy, and ship's biscuit was the first of the three Bs that made up the seaman's diet of Biscuit, Beer, & Beef. "One pound . . . of good, clean sweet, sound, well-bolted with a horse-cloth, well-baked, and well-conditioned wheaten biscuit; one gallon . . . of beer . . . two pounds . . . of beef, killed and made up with salt in England, of a well-fed ox . . . for Sundays, Mondays, Tuesdays, and Thursdays." And while one gallon of beer might seem excessive, it was a low-alcohol beer called small beer and wasn't likely to get anyone drunk. That was what the rum was for, though even that was often watered down to make grog.

The reason hardtack was a perfect military food was that, with its low to nonexistent water content, it was the only way to keep bread from getting moldy and could sit in a barrel for months or even years and still be good enough to eat. That's if bugs didn't get to it first. Biscuits were definitely less attractive to bugs than fresh bread or uncooked flour, but on a ship a worm would take what it could get. In *The Adventures of Roderick Random* by Tobias Smollett in 1748, in describing the rations aboard a ship, it says "every biscuit whereof, like a piece of clockwork, moved by its own internal impulse, occasioned by the myriads of insects that dwelt within it . . ." This is, no doubt, where the term "worm castles" came from. So even though I'm sure your sea biscuits will be safe from infestation in your own home, I'd keep them in an airtight container all the same.

MAKES 6 LARGE BISCUITS
COOK TIME: 7 HOURS 20 MINUTES

4 cups (450 g) whole wheat flour

1 cup (235 ml) water

1. Preheat the oven to 300°F/150°C.

2. In a large bowl mix the flour with ½ cup of the water. Mix until combined, then begin adding the rest of the water 1 tablespoon at a time. Once the flour comes together to form a dough, stop adding water; you will likely not require the full cup. Once you have a dry dough, knead it until it's smooth, about 15 minutes. Divide the kneaded dough into 6 equal pieces.

3. Form each piece of dough into a ball, then gently roll them into rounds ½ inch thick. They should look like English muffins. Place

the biscuits on a lined baking sheet and poke small holes all over the top of each, as you would a cracker. Set the baking sheet in the oven and bake for 3 hours. The biscuits should easily come away from the sheet at this time. Leave them in the oven and reduce the temperature to 200°F/95°C for 3 or 4 more hours, or until the biscuits are rock hard.

4. These ship's biscuits, or hardtack, are not meant to be eaten in this state, at least if you value your teeth. They are meant to either be soaked in water or beer before being eaten or else broken with a hammer, then used as an ingredient to thicken stew.

Stobhach Gaedhealach (Irish Stew)

City/Region: Ireland
Time Period: c. 1900

FROM HISTORY

Stobhach Gaedhealach—Put a layer of potatoes in the pot, a layer of meat on top of that, onions, salt and pepper, and so on until the pot is full. Have a layer of potatoes on top. Pour in the water and turn on the fire. Let it boil, pull it to the side, and let it simmer an hour and a half. Take it up; put the meat in the middle, the potatoes around it and the gravy down on it.

—Sisters of Mercy, Callan, Ireland, *Leabhar cócaireachta*[1]

The Potato Harvest by Winifred Knights

Ever since being introduced to the Emerald Isle by Sir Walter Raleigh in 1589, the potato has been a staple of the Irish diet, and no Irish stew would be complete without them. But in 1845 this important crop fell victim to blight, leading to one of the worst famines in European history:

> *The leaves of the potatoes on many fields I passed were quite withered, and a strange stench, such as I had never smelt before, but which became a well-known feature in "the blight" for years after, filled the atmosphere adjoining each field of potatoes. . . . The crop of all crops, on which they depended for food, had suddenly melted away.*
>
> —William Steuart Trench, a County Cork land agent, *Realities of Irish Life*

Over the next two years, three-quarters of the potato crop failed. As Ireland was part of the British Empire, the Irish depended on the English government for assistance, but that assistance was put in the hands of Charles Trevelyan, who had a less than generous view of those he was meant to help:

> *The judgment of God sent the calamity to teach the Irish a lesson, that calamity must not be too much mitigated. . . . The real evil with which we have to contend is not the physical evil of the Famine, but the moral evil of the selfish, perverse, and turbulent character of the people.*

continues

Stobhach Gaedhealach (Irish Stew)

continued

With little help from their government, the Irish people depended on the charity of other nations and private citizens. Donations came in from the tsar of Russia, the sultan of the Ottoman Empire, the pope, the city of Calcutta, Queen Victoria, the United States, and a young congressman named Abraham Lincoln. One of the most famous donations, a gift of $170, came in 1847 from the Choctaw Nation, who only sixteen years before had experienced starvation themselves on the infamous Trail of Tears. The Society of Friends, also known as the Quakers, sent tons of food from the United States and founded soup kitchens throughout Ireland, though their ability to help was dwarfed by the enormity of the situation. Sadly, for many, the choice was starvation or emigration. Between 1845 and 1851, over a million people perished and an estimated half million fled the country, mostly settling in Canada and the United States. By the end of the century, the population of Ireland had fallen from 8 million to 4.5 million, and, to this day, it has never fully recovered. So, as you enjoy a warm bowl of *stobhach gaedhealach*, spare a thought for those lives upended by the loss of its main ingredient.

MAKES 4 TO 6 SERVINGS   **COOK TIME:** 1 HOUR 45 MINUTES

3 pounds (1.4 kg) floury potatoes, such as russet

½ pound (225 g) trimmed lamb shank, cut in bite-size pieces

¼ pound (115 g) Irish or Danish bacon (or substitute Canadian bacon), chopped into ½-inch pieces

2 large yellow or white onions, finely chopped

1½ teaspoons sea salt

1½ teaspoons freshly ground black pepper

10 ounces (300 ml) water

Additional salt and pepper, to taste

1. Wash and peel the potatoes, then chop them into large, bite-size chunks.

2. Place half of the potatoes in a layer on the bottom of a large pot or Dutch oven. Then place a layer of the combined lamb and bacon on top of the potatoes. Next, layer the onions over the meat. Sprinkle the salt and pepper over the onion layer. Use the remaining potatoes as a final layer, on top of the onions. (If you are using a pot that's on the smaller side, you can make multiple layers following the order given.) Pour water over the top layer. You may be tempted to add more, but it's not necessary at this point.

3. Set the pot over high heat and bring to a boil. Once it is boiling, turn the heat down to medium low and cover the pot. Simmer until the potatoes are soft, 60 to 90 minutes. From time to time, check on the stew to make sure there is still water bubbling up between the potatoes. Only add water if the stew is close to going dry. Unlike most modern stews, this will have little broth, but some liquid is necessary to keep the stew from burning to the bottom of the pot.

An Irish Peasant Family Discovering the Blight of Their Store by Daniel Macdonald

The stew should not need stirring but can be if you wish. When the stew is cooked to your liking, serve hot, adding additional salt and pepper, to taste.

If you'd ask a young lover to dine,
And have him prove kind unto you,
To make love come out of his beautiful mouth
You should stuff it with Irish stew.
Then Hurrah for an Irish stew,
That will stick to your belly like glue,
It's season'd so fine, and its flavour's divine,
Och! Good luck to an Irish stew.
—Melodist, and Mirthful Olio (1828)

Simnel Cake

City/Region: England
Time Period: 1914

FROM HISTORY

Take a quarter of a pound of flour, three ounces of mixed peel, quarter of a pound of butter, three good-sized eggs, quarter of a pound of castor sugar, two ounces of ground almonds, three-quarters of a pound of currants. Beat butter to a cream, add sugar and beaten eggs gradually, and work well together. Add flour sifted; beat thoroughly, then add remaining ingredients. Line a tin with greased paper, pour in mixture, and bake in gentle oven from two to three hours. When cold, make some almond paste. Put a layer on top of cake. Form remainder into round balls. Brush the cake over with white of egg and dust with castor sugar. Set in a cool oven till balls are lightly browned, and decorate with crystallized fruits.

—May Byron, *Pot-luck; or, The British Home Cookery Book*

Simnel cake is a traditional English treat served on Mothering Sunday, which originally had nothing to do with mothers. It was the day set aside each spring to visit your mother church, or where you were baptized. At a time when people tended to live in their hometowns all their lives, this often meant going to the same church you always went to, not too exciting. But in the eighteenth and nineteenth centuries, as people flocked from rural villages to industrial jobs in the cities, the yearly pilgrimage home made a good excuse to visit your actual mother as well. And when you visit Mom, you should bring a simnel cake.

But how did the simnel cake get its name? Sounds like something that didn't make it into Rudyard Kipling's *Just So Stories*. But just as the Victorian Kipling offered an incredible explanation of how the elephant got its trunk, so did other Victorian authors offer incredible stories of how the simnel got its name.

First up is the story of a pretender to the English throne. After defeating Richard III at the Battle of Bosworth Field in 1485, Henry Tudor had himself crowned Henry VII. But before he could settle into the royal life, a boy of ten came forward claiming that he was Edward, Earl of Warwick, and the true heir to the throne. He was not. His name was Lambert Simnel and he had zero claim to the throne. But that didn't stop him, and those using him as a pawn against the new king, Henry VII, from leading an army into battle at Stoke Field, where he was quickly defeated. His adult handlers were either imprisoned or executed. But Simnel, being only ten, was sent to work in the royal kitchens as a spit turner. It was there that he allegedly invented a cake, which they named after him. Simnel cake. A wonderful story, but absolutely hogwash, since the cake had been around long before he was born. In fact, his name, Simnel, likely came from the fact that someone in his family's past had been a baker who took the name Simnel after the bread of the same name.

Now, the story of wee Simnel does at least have some history behind it. The other Victorian fabrication does not. It's documented in *Chambers' Book of Days*, which was a miscellany that included histories, anecdotes, "and Oddities of Human Life and Character."

In the 1867 edition, there is a story of a couple, Simon and Nelly (who conveniently go by Sim and Nell, if you didn't see where this was going). Near the end of Lent, they come across a bit of unleavened dough that needs using up and Nel proposes they make a cake. Sim goes along with the plan, but

when the cake was made, a subject of violent discord arose, Sim insisting that it should be boiled, while Nell no less obstinately contended that it should be baked. The dispute ran from words to blows, for Nell, not choosing to let her province in the household be thus interfered with, jumped up, and threw the stool she was sitting on at Sim, who on his part seized a besom, and applied it with right good will to the head and shoulders of his spouse. Now she seized the broom, and the battle became so warm, that it might have had a very serious result, had not Nell proposed a compromise that the cake should be boiled first, and afterwards baked.

I learned a new word when reading this: "besom." It turns out to be one of those brooms made of twigs tied to the end of a stick, a true witch's

continues

Simnel Cake

continued

broom, which I've always thought seemed highly impractical for actually sweeping.

So this boiled and then baked cake took on the name Sim-Nel or simnel cake. Another clear fabrication, but a story you'll still hear kicking around church cake sales around Easter.

In actuality, the name simnel likely comes from the Latin *simila conspersa*, meaning "fine white flour," and originally referred to white bread. Rather unexciting as far as history goes, which is probably why the Victorians decided to make up something else.

MAKES ONE 8-INCH CAKE **COOK TIME:** 3 HOURS 30 MINUTES

FOR CAKE:
2 cups (340 g) dried currants (see page 12)

8 tablespoons (115 g) salted butter at room temperature, plus more for greasing

1 cup (120 g) all-purpose flour

1½ teaspoons baking powder

1 teaspoon kosher salt

½ heaping cup (110 g) baker's sugar

3 large eggs at room temperature

½ cup (60 g) almond flour

½ cup (85 g) mixed peel

FOR ALMOND PASTE AND TOPPING:
1¼ cups (250 g) baker's sugar, plus 1 tablespoon for dusting

2½ cups (250 g) almond flour

1 large egg, plus 1 large egg white, divided

Candied fruit or other confections, if desired

1. Preheat oven to 300°F/150°C. Set oven rack in the middle of the oven.

2. Soak the currants in cool water for 30 minutes to rehydrate. Then drain.

3. Line the bottom of an 8-inch cake pan with parchment and butter the sides of the pan.

4. In a medium bowl, whisk the flour, baking powder, and salt together.

5. In a large bowl, beat the butter until light and fluffy. Gradually beat in the sugar and then the 3 eggs until incorporated. Sift the almond flour into the egg and sugar mixture and gently fold into the batter. Sift the whisked flour mixture into the bowl and gently fold into the batter. Add the mixed peel and currants and mix until incorporated, being careful not to overmix.

6. Spoon the batter into the prepared pan and smooth the top with a spatula. Bake for 1 hour or until a wooden skewer inserted into the middle comes out clean. Remove the cake from the oven and set it on a wire rack to cool for 15 minutes, then remove the cake from the pan and allow to cool completely, at least 2 hours.

7. Make the almond paste: Mix the sugar and almond flour together in a medium bowl. Add 1 egg and mix until you have a smooth paste. Divide the paste into thirds. Two-thirds should be combined and formed into one disk, then wrapped in cling film. Then the remaining ⅓ of the paste can be preformed into balls. Refrigerate for 1 hour or longer.

8. Once the paste is chilled, roll the larger almond paste disk between two parchment sheets into a disk 8 to 9 inches in diameter and approximately ¼ inch thick. To get a precise circle, place a clean baking pan on top of the rolled-out paste, trace lightly with a skewer around the bottom of the pan to create a circle, then cut out with a sharp knife. Set on top of the cooled cake. The paste can be scored in a diamond pattern, making sure not to cut fully through the paste, and/or the edges can be crimped for decoration. Take the other third of the almond paste and form 11 small balls and set them in a large circle on top of the cake.

9. Brush the almond paste with the egg white and lightly dust with baker's sugar. Set the cake on a lined baking sheet and return it to the top oven rack with the lowest broiler setting for 2 to 4 minutes or until lightly brown. If the color is uneven, turn the pan. Keep a close eye, as it can easily burn. Alternately, use a baking torch to caramelize the sugar.

10. Decorate the finished cake with candied fruit, if desired, or other confections and serve.

CONTINENTAL EUROPE

✕✕✕

Lasagne

✕✕✕✕✕✕✕✕✕✕✕✕✕✕

City/Region: Italy
Time Period: c. 1300

FROM HISTORY

To make lasagne take leavened paste and make a shape as thin as you can. Then divide it into squares the size of three fingers. After that, take boiled salted water and cook the lasagne in it. And when they are well boiled, add grated cheese.

And if you like, you can combine good quality spiced powders and powder them on when they are on the plate. Put down a layer of lasagne and powder again, and another layer and powder, and on until the bowl or plate be full. Afterwards, eat them with a wooden skewer.

—*Liber de coquina*

The origin of lasagne is unknown. Etymologically, it likely comes from the Ancient Greek word *laganon*, which referred to flat sheets of thin dough cut into strips. Though some believe it came from the Latin *lasanum*, which referred to a type of pot that the pasta was boiled or served in. But regardless of the Greek or Roman origin of the name, the dish itself almost definitely has its roots in Ancient Rome. Patinam Apicianam sic facies and Patina a la Apicius are layered dishes found in Apicius's *De re coquinaria*, the cookbook from which so many of the recipes in the Ancient Roman section of this book come. These *patina* were a cross between a modern lasagne and middle school Sloppy Joes, though the ingredients include things like turtledove and sow's udder, which I guess is also like middle school Sloppy Joes.

By the medieval era, when our recipe was written, the lasagne had become something closer to what we would recognize today, though still unbaked and with no sauce of any kind, let alone tomato sauce, which wouldn't come to Italian food until the 1500s. But even in its early form, the dish had become a staple of Italian cuisine and is written of often even

Opposite: A page from *Liber de coquina*

Above: *Saint Sebastian Interceding for the Plague Stricken* by Josse Lieferinxe

outside of cookbooks. The thirteenth-century Franciscan friar Jacopone da Todi wrote: "Those who count only size are often deceived. The strength of a grain of pepper will conquer lasagne." Something to keep in mind when we pepper our lasagne.

Another medieval writer, Baldassarre Bonaiuti, gives us an idea of how to distribute the cheese on the lasagne in his *Florentine Chronicle* (1348), though he does this by detailing how plague victims were dealt with during the Black Death:

> *Dirt would be taken and thrown down on them; and then more bodies would come on top of them, and then more dirt on top again, they put layer on layer, with very little dirt between them, like putting layers of cheese in a lasagne.*

Macabre, but useful in knowing that this lasagne shouldn't be as densely cheesy as the modern version, nor the cheesy *Tourte of Lasagne* that Bartolomeo Scappi lays out in his *Opera*. That version, from the Italian Renaissance, includes both Provatura and Parmesan as well as a healthy amount of butter and spices.

Now, there is one lasagne myth that I must put to bed here and now, and that is the erroneous claim that it was the English who actually invented lasagne. This idea comes from the fact that, in the 1390s, a recipe for lasagne under the name *loseyn* appears in *The Forme of Cury*. While it's remarkable to find a lasagne recipe this early in England, it is at least fifty years later than the one from *Liber de coquina* that we are using as our template here. The recipes are strikingly similar, with the major exception that the Italian recipe includes yeasted dough, an outlier among all medieval recipes for lasagne, but one that should make the dish quite interesting.

continues

Lasagne

continued

½ teaspoon ground grains of paradise (see page 12) or black pepper

½ teaspoon ground ginger

¼ teaspoon ground cinnamon

¼ teaspoon ground nutmeg

⅛ teaspoon ground clove

2 teaspoons (7 g) dried yeast

1 cup (235 ml) warm water, divided

3 cups (360 g) bread flour

1 teaspoon sea salt, plus more for boiling

Drizzle of extra-virgin olive oil

8 ounces (226 g) hard cheese, such as Pecorino Romano or Parmesan, grated

MAKES 4 SERVINGS **COOK TIME:** 1 HOUR 45 MINUTES

1. Prepare the spice mixture by whisking the grains of paradise or black pepper, ginger, cinnamon, nutmeg, and clove together and set aside. The recipe is not specific in what spices should be used, so feel free to alter the mixture in any way you like. Other recipes specifically call for *powder douce*, which was sweet and would include sugar, and others rely more heavily on the pepper to darken the flavor.

2. Dissolve the yeast into ¼ cup of the warm water and leave to proof for 10 minutes. Once the yeast is active, stir it into the flour mixture, then add the remaining ¾ cup water and the teaspoon of salt to form a dough. Once the dough comes together, knead it for 15 minutes or until the dough is smooth and elastic, then set in a bowl and cover, letting it rise for 1 hour.

3. Once the dough has risen, punch it down and roll it out on a lightly floured surface into a large, thin sheet. The pasta should be between ⅟₁₆ and ⅛ inch thick. Depending on your work-space size, it might be easiest to divide the dough in half or thirds before rolling it out. Cut the dough into squares three fingers across and set aside.

4. Bring a large pot of salted water to a boil over high heat and add a drizzle of olive oil to help keep the pasta from sticking to itself. Once the water is boiling, add the pasta to the pot and boil for 3 or 4 minutes, stirring occasionally to keep it from sticking. You'll know that it is done when it rises to the surface of the water.

5. Remove the lasagne from the pot using a slotted spoon and set it on a plate while you assemble the lasagne. Working quickly, while the pasta is still warm, line the bottom of a dish with a single layer of pasta, then sprinkle with a layer of cheese and a small amount of the spices. Continue this until you've three layers of each, topping the lasagne with cheese and spices. Then serve hot.

Black Porée

XXXXXXXXXXXXXXXXXX

City/Region: France
Time Period: c. 1393

FROM HISTORY

Black porée is the one made with slices of grilled salt pork; that is to say the porée is trimmed, washed, chopped up, then blanched in boiling water, then fried in the pork fat; and then thinned with the boiling water (It's said if it is washed with cold water, it would be uglier and darker), then it is advisable to put two pieces of pork upon each bowl.

—*Le Ménagier de Paris*

Harvesting cabbage from
Tacuinum Sanitatis

Most of the medieval recipes in this book are rather hoity-toity. Since they come from cookbooks, which were mostly written for the wealthy, it only makes sense that the dishes are rife with expensive cuts of meat, game that was only available to the wealthy, or chock-full of precious spices from the Orient like nutmeg, clove, or even sugar. But I thought I should include at least one recipe that the peasants, likely my ancestors, could have eaten. And to do so, I knew exactly where to look.

Le Ménagier de Paris was written around 1393 and is written in the fictional voice of an elderly husband instructing his new wife, a girl of fifteen, on how to manage the household. This includes, among other things, gardening tips, instructions for when she visits the market, advice on how to keep her husband satisfied in the bedroom, and of course recipes, including three for *porée*.

Porée is a simple dish of cooked greens, and the book includes recipes for white *porée* made with leeks, green *porée* made with cheese or butter, and black *porée* made with bacon fat. All three could have been cooked by most peasant families, but the pork fat won me over when I was deciding which to include here. It's also the simplest and thus the one most suited to a peasant family making ends meet.

Provided they had a small cottage for which they paid rent to their lord, they likely had a small garden attached. There they could grow fresh greens as well as an assortment of herbs both for flavoring their food and for use as medicine. A pig would have been more expensive, but even so, most families could afford, or were given, at least one small pig each year, which they would raise, then slaughter and smoke or salt the meat for the winter. When it comes to salt, there are many misconceptions about that ingredient and its cost throughout history. Entire books have been written on the subject (check out *Salt: A World History* by Mark Kurlansky) and this isn't one of those books, but while quality salt could be prohibitively expensive at times, it was often available to all even if the quality was substandard. Of course, if you lived near the ocean, getting your own salt was quite simple, but most peasants in Europe didn't have that option. But I digress. The greens, pork, and salt were all something most people could get their hands on, making this a perfect peasant dish.

MAKES 4 SERVINGS   **COOK TIME:** 45 MINUTES

8 ounces (225 g) fatty salted pork belly

3 pounds (1.5 kg) chard, or similar green vegetable

Water

Salt to taste

1. Chop the pork belly into several large pieces. Put the pork in a large saucepan set over low heat. Allow the fat to slowly melt while you prepare the chard, about 3 minutes.

2. Meanwhile, bring a large pot of water to a boil. Wash the chard, remove any white parts from the stem, and slice the leaves into long, 1-inch-wide strips. Put the chard in water and return it to a boil. Cook for 15 seconds, then remove the pot from the stove, drain the chard, and dry it as much as possible.

3. Once the chard is dry and the pork fat has been rendered, raise the saucepan's heat to medium low and toss the chard with the pork, coating it in pork fat. Cook, uncovered, for 15 minutes, tossing the greens occasionally.

4. Bring 2 cups (450 ml) of water to a boil in a small saucepan. Once the chard has cooked for 15 minutes, pour the boiling water over the chard and simmer for 5 to 10 minutes. Add salt to taste. Serve the greens with any unrendered pieces of pork on top.

A Tart of Apples

✕✕✕✕✕✕✕✕✕✕✕✕✕✕✕✕

City/Region: Germany
Time Period: c. 1553

American Cookery by
Amelia Simmons

W hile you may have heard the phrase "American as apple pie," this sixteenth-century recipe from Germany got there first. Though it was written nearly two centuries after the first English recipe, which combined apples, pears, and figs. Other early European recipes called for the apples to be mashed into a sauce, then mixed with cream before being baked, and one, from this same German cookbook, mixed the apples with cheese. With so many recipes across so many countries, it's clear that Europe's love for apple pie long predates their trips to the New World.

In fact, the first American mention of the pie didn't come until October 1, 1697, when the judge Samuel Sewall, most famous for presiding over the Salem Witch Trials, wrote in his journal of a picnic on Hog Island where he "had first Butter, Honey, Curds and Cream. For Diner, very good Rost Lamb, Turkey, Fowls, Aplepy." But new as it was, the dessert caught on quickly here, and when the eighteenth-century Lutheran missionary Dr. Israel Acrelius of Sweden arrived in the colony of New Sweden in Delaware, he remarked: "Apple pie is used throughout the whole year, and when fresh Apples are no longer to be had, dried ones are used. It is the evening meal of children. House pie, in country places, is made of Apples neither peeled nor freed from their cores, and its crust is not broken if a wagon wheel goes over it" (*A History of New Sweden*).

Not a particularly flattering description, and with the reputation of American apple pie trod in the mud, it was up to Amelia Simmons to clean it up. In America's first cookbook, from 1796, *American Cookery*, Ms. Simmons offers two recipes for apple pie with rosewater, a popular ingredient in much baking of the period. But even with these spruced-up recipes, apple pie's association with Americanness had another 150 years to wait. Not until the GIs of WW II headed across the Atlantic to fight in Germany did "mom and apple pie" become something to fight for. In light of that, I suppose it's somewhat ironic that this apple pie recipe is German, but I assure you, it's no less delicious.

MAKES ONE 9-INCH PIE   **COOK TIME:** 3 HOURS

FOR THE PASTRY:
3 cups all-purpose flour

1 teaspoon kosher salt

8 tablespoons (113 g) cold, unsalted butter

3 large egg yolks

½ cup (120 ml) ice water

FOR THE FILLING:
8 medium apples

8 tablespoons (113 g) salted butter, divided

3 large egg yolks

1½ teaspoon ground cinnamon

½ cup (100 g) granulated sugar

½ teaspoon ground ginger

FOR THE EGG WASH:
1 large egg white

1 tablespoon water

1. Make the pastry: In a medium bowl, whisk together the flour and salt, then cut the butter into ½-inch pieces and work the butter into the flour with your fingertips until you get a crumbly texture. Add the egg yolks and work them into the dough until incorporated. Then add the water, one tablespoon at a time, until the dough comes together. Do not use any more water than is necessary. Divide the dough into two pieces, one slightly larger than the other. Wrap each piece in plastic wrap and refrigerate for at least 1 hour, but preferably overnight.

2. Once the dough has rested, remove the larger piece from the refrigerator and let it sit for 5 minutes, then roll it out on a lightly floured surface into a 13-inch circle. Lightly grease a pie pan and line it with the larger circle of pastry. Trim it, leaving one inch overhanging the pan all around the edge. Cover and return to the refrigerator while you prepare the filling.

3. Preheat the oven to 425°F/220°C.

4. Make the filling: Peel and core the apples, then cut them into thick slices, about 8 per apple. Melt 2 tablespoons of butter in a pan over medium heat and add the apple slices, frying them until soft, about 10 minutes. Continue to flip them so that they cook evenly. Then remove them from the heat and let them cool.

5. Once the apple slices are cooled, cut each one into ½-inch pieces. Whisk the egg yolks in a bowl, then add the apple pieces, coating them in the yolks. Melt the remaining 6 tablespoons of butter in the saucepan, then remove it from the heat and add the cinnamon, sugar, and ginger and stir until well combined. Pour the mixture over the apples and coat them well, then set aside for 5 minutes.

continues

A Tart of Apples

continued

6. Remove the pie pan and the rest of the pastry from the refrigerator. Spoon the apples into the lined pan. Roll the remaining pastry into an 11-inch circle and lay it over the apples. Bring the overlapping bottom crust up over the top crust and pinch to seal all the way around, making a decorative crimp. Cut 4 to 6 holes in the top of the crust to allow steam to vent. Alternatively, a lattice crust works well for this pie. Make an egg wash of 1 egg white and a tablespoon of water whisked together in small bowl. Lightly brush the top with the egg wash. Place the pie in the refrigerator for 15 minutes.

7. After the pie has been refrigerated, set it on a lined baking sheet and bake for 20 minutes, then reduce the oven temperature to 375°F/190°C and bake an additional 40 minutes, or until the filling is bubbling up through the top. If the edge of the pie begins to darken too quickly, cover with a pie shield.

8. Remove the pie from the oven and let it cool completely before serving.

Samuel Sewall by John Smibert

Torta d'Herbe Communi

✕✕✕✕✕✕✕✕✕✕✕✕✕✕✕

City/Region: Italy
Time Period: 1570

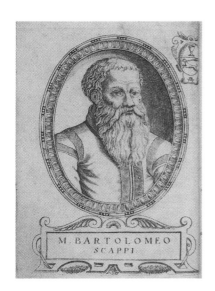

Bartolomeo Scappi

artolomeo Scappi was the closest thing to a celebrity chef that Renaissance Italy had to offer. As the chef to the Papal court, his name was famous throughout the kitchens of Europe, and in 1570 his recipes became famous too. After a career cooking for the Vatican's elite, he published *Opera dell'arte del cucinare*, better known as Scappi's *Opera*, which included over one thousand recipes.

Composed of six books, the *Opera* opens with an imagined chat between the chef and his apprentice, Giovanni, where Scappi instructs him how best to run a kitchen and what it takes to be a great chef:

He must be alert, patient and modest in everything he
does, and as sober as possible because whoever is without
a good deal of sobriety loses patience as well as a natural
taste for things.[2]

continues

Torta d'Herbe Communi

continued

(Having worked with a number of excellent chefs in my life, I feel Scappi's advice often falls on deaf ears.)

He then describes how to equip an Italian Renaissance kitchen, accompanied by detailed images of the kitchens and implements used at the time, including the first known image of a fork. But nothing was more important than "a cabinet ten hands high and six wide, with several compartments that can all be locked holding sugars, spices and other things used daily in the personal food of the Prince."[3]

These spices and sugar were the hallmark of Scappi's cooking. As seen by the quantities of spices in the recipe for the herb torte, he used them liberally and in combinations we might think odd today. The potency of the spices may have been less than we are used to, due to poor storage and a long transportation, something I allow for in the modern recipe. With few exceptions, sugar today is relegated to dessert and a few sauces and salad dressings, but Scappi includes it in nine hundred of his one thousand recipes. The concept of sweet and savory being kept separate during a meal wouldn't come about for nearly a century.

The other five books of the *Opera* are the recipes themselves, many of which hint at dishes we are familiar with today. An early pumpkin pie, the first European recipes for turkey, better known then as the Indian Peacock, and a black grape sauce for roast duck that would be comfortable on any modern menu. But he also includes recipes for hedgehog, piglet, porcupine, bear, and sweet sugared bull testicles. I decided to include the common herb torte recipe in this cookbook rather than one of Scappi's more signature dishes; you're welcome.

MAKES ONE 9-INCH TORTA
COOK TIME: 2 HOURS 45 MINUTES

**FOR THE PASTRY
(SEE COOK'S NOTE):**
3 cups (385 g) all-purpose flour

2 teaspoons kosher salt

1½ cups (340 g) unsalted butter, chilled and cut into ¼-inch pieces

¾ cup (177 ml) cold water, divided

1. Make the pastry (if using store-bought dough, divide it into two pieces, comprising two-thirds and one-third portions, and skip to step 2): Mix the flour and salt in a large bowl, and add the butter and lightly coat the pieces with flour. Using your fingers, rub the butter into the flour until pea-sized pieces of butter remain. Quickly mix in ½ cup of the cold water, until you have a rough but firm dough. Add in the remaining water little by little, only if needed. Cover with plastic wrap and refrigerate for 30 minutes, or until the dough is firm enough to roll.

FOR THE FILLING:
¾ pound (340 g) ricotta cheese

½ pound (225 g) Parmesan cheese

½ cup (115 g) mascarpone

3 large eggs

6 tablespoons (85 g) salted butter, softened

½ cup (100 g) granulated sugar

2 tablespoons finely chopped fresh mint

2 tablespoons finely chopped fresh marjoram

1½ tablespoons ground cinnamon

1 tablespoon freshly ground black pepper

1½ teaspoons ground cloves

2 cups finely chopped chard

2 cups finely chopped spinach

FOR THE EGG WASH:
1 large egg

1 tablespoon water

2. On a lightly floured surface, gently knead the dough, just until it comes together. Form it into a 12-inch (30 cm) square. Roll the dough in one direction until you have a rectangle about 30 x 16 inches (91 x 40 cm). The butter should leave marbled streaks through the dough. Fold the top third of the dough into the center and the bottom third over that. Turn the dough 90 degrees and roll out again, as before. Then fold in thirds a second time. Divide the dough into two pieces, one piece being two-thirds of the dough and the other one-third. Wrap each piece in plastic wrap and refrigerate for 20 minutes.

3. Preheat the oven to 375°F/190°C. Using butter or nonstick cooking spray, lightly grease a 9-inch springform or removable-bottom cake pan.

4. On a floured work surface, roll the larger portion of pastry out into a rough 15-inch circle, about ¼ inch thick. Transfer it to the prepared cake pan. Allow an inch of dough to overhang the pan's edge to prevent the crust from sagging while blind baking. Trim any dough in excess of the 1-inch overhang and set it aside to patch any cracks that may arise during blind baking. Refrigerate the dough-lined pan for 20 minutes.

5. Roll the remaining pastry into a 10-inch circle and return to the refrigerator.

6. Line the chilled crust with parchment and fill completely with pie weights, gently pressing the weights into the corners of the shell. Set it on a rimmed baking sheet and bake on the lower-middle oven rack for 30 minutes, or until the edges begin to brown. Remove it from the oven, and carefully remove the parchment and pie weights. Return the empty crust to the oven for 15 minutes, or until the bottom is lightly browned all over. Remove the crust from the oven and allow to cool on a wire rack. Reduce oven temperature to 350°F/180°C.

7. Make the filling: Mix the ricotta, Parmesan, and mascarpone in a large bowl until combined and few lumps remain. Add the eggs and beat until incorporated. Then add the butter, sugar, mint, marjoram, cinnamon, pepper, and cloves and mix until combined. Finally, mix in the chard and spinach by hand, so as not to bruise the greens. Once the filling is well mixed, pour it into the cooled pastry shell and

continues

Torta d'Herbe Communi

continued

smooth the top. The filling should reach almost to the top of the crust.

8. Remove the 10-inch circle of pastry from the refrigerator and use it to cover the top of the torta, tucking it between the filling and outer shell. Do not tuck it too tightly; leave some ripples on the top to give room for the filling to expand during baking. Cut a small hole in the center of the torta to allow steam to escape.

9. Make the egg wash: Whisk the egg and water together until very smooth. Brush the top of the torta with the egg wash, then set it on the bottom rack of the oven and bake for 1 hour, until the crust is browned. Once the torta is baked, remove from the oven and allow to cool for 15 minutes, then slice and serve warm.

Cook's Note: This pastry mimics several of Scappi's pastries, but a modern puff pastry will work as well.

Pumpkin Tourte

City/Region: Italy
Time Period: 1570

This recipe for a pumpkin tourte is one of the first recipes for pumpkin anything in Europe. The gourd had only arrived from the New World a few decades earlier and Bartolomeo Scappi was one of the first chefs to put it to work. The pumpkin he would have used is unknown and was likely several different varieties, none of which we have today, but a sugar pumpkin or butternut squash gives the best flavor here.

This recipe is a favorite of mine for two reasons: One, it is without a shell, that is, crustless, and I often feel crusts take up valuable real estate that could be used for more filling. Two, while the word Scappi uses to describe it is "tourte," the word I'd use is "cheesecake." The first pumpkin cheesecake, though far from the first cheesecake of any kind.

As far back as 2000 BC, the inhabitants of the isle of Samos were dining on a savory cheesecake that they used for weddings and religious festivals. By 776 BC, those cheesecakes were eaten by Greek athletes preparing for the first Olympic games, which makes me wonder why there isn't a Cheesecake

Factory in the Olympic Village. By the Romans' Republic, the cheesecake had become sweetened with honey, like in the recipe for placenta by Cato the Elder. He also has recipes for cheesecakes called Libum and Savillum, the latter of which begins to resemble the cheesecakes of later millennia, and perhaps it was one of those that some Roman settler brought to Britannia, for cheesecake has been a staple there for centuries.

In *The Forme of Cury* (c. 1390) the chefs of Richard II give us a recipe for Sambocade, a cheesecake flavored with elderflower. The filling is not all that different from Scappi's pumpkin tourte two centuries later, except that Scappi is more specific in his choices of cheese and loads up on the spices, as he was known to do. In this recipe, the amount of cinnamon that he calls for is so much that it becomes overwhelming to the point of unpalatable. That is likely because, in the sixteenth century, cinnamon and other spices took a very long time to travel from the Orient to Vatican City and when it got there it was stored in a wooden chest of drawers or metal box rather than tightly sealed bottles like we use today. With that in mind, I've cut back on the cinnamon quantity to better emulate what I think Scappi intended in this, the first recipe for pumpkin cheesecake.

MAKES ONE 9-INCH TOURTE
COOK TIME: 6 HOURS 30 MINUTES

FOR THE PUMPKIN PUREE:
2 quarts (2 liters) beef broth or 2 quarts (2 liters) water

2 tablespoons salted butter

1 tablespoon kosher salt

1 (3- to 5-pound) (1.25 to 2.25 kg) pumpkin or squash (see Cook's Note)

1. Preheat the oven to 350°F/175°C.

2. Make the pumpkin puree: Heat the beef broth or water with the butter and salt in a large pot over high heat. Chop the stem and bottom off the pumpkin, then slice the pumpkin in two. Peel each half and remove the seeds and any stringy bits. Cut the pumpkin into small pieces 1 to 1½ inches (2.5 to 3.5 cm) square. Once the broth or water is boiling, add the pumpkin and boil for 20 minutes or until easily skewered with a knife.

3. Strain the pumpkin into a colander, then mash or blend the pumpkin into a smooth puree. Place a fine-mesh sieve over a large pot and transfer the puree to the sieve and let the liquid drain from the puree for 5 minutes. You can gently stir the puree to release more liquid, but do not press the puree through the sieve.

continues

Pumpkin Tourte

continued

FOR THE FILLING:
1 cup (240 g) ricotta cheese

1 cup (225 g) mascarpone or cream cheese

6 large eggs

1¼ cups (250 g) light brown sugar

2 tablespoons ground cinnamon

4 teaspoons ground ginger

1 teaspoon kosher salt

½ cup (120 ml) whole milk

4 tablespoons (55 g) unsalted butter

2 tablespoons (30 g) salted butter

FOR THE TOPPING:
1 tablespoon granulated sugar

1 teaspoon ground cinnamon

4. Make the filling: Once the puree is drained, put it in a medium bowl and mix in the ricotta and mascarpone until smooth. Whisk the eggs separately, then add them to the bowl with the pumpkin and mix until fully incorporated. Add the brown sugar, cinnamon, ginger, and salt and mix. Finally, pour in the milk and the 4 tablespoons of unsalted butter and beat the mixture until smooth.

5. Melt the salted butter in a small saucepan over medium heat, then pour it into a deep pie pan or cake pan and roll it around the pan to coat the bottom and sides. Pour the pumpkin filling into the pan. Mix the sugar and cinnamon, then sprinkle it on top of the tourte.

6. Set the tourte on the middle rack of the oven and bake until the filling has puffed up and there is a slight wobble in the center, about 1 hour and 15 minutes. Turn off the oven and allow the cheesecake to stay in the oven to slowly cool for another 45 minutes. Then remove it from the oven and set it on a cooling rack to cool completely, about 4 hours. Do not cut the tourte until it is fully cooled. If it is to be served warm, reheat it in a low oven for 15 minutes.

Cook's Note: The pumpkin will be used to make 2 cups of puree. Alternatively, use 2 cups (450 g) canned pumpkin.

Beef with Garlic Harvester Sauce

City/Region: Transylvania
Time Period: 1580

> ### FROM HISTORY
>
> *Beef with Garlic Harvester Sauce*
> *Do the same. What we call garlic harvest*
> *sauce, as I said, is that you beat eggs in vinegar,*
> *peel the garlic clove by clove, break it well, add*
> *it to the eggs and vinegar; then dilute it (add*
> *broth or vinegar) as I said before. Break it well*
> *with the blanching stick after adding liquid,*
> *be careful to keep it from shrinking.*
>
> —The Prince of Transylvania's Court Cookbook
> (translated by Bence Kovacs)[1]

This dish comes from a collection of recipes by the master chef at the Prince of Transylvania's court, and as it's written conversationally, often referring to other recipes in the book, there is a great deal of guesswork that goes into re-creating it. What is for sure is that the cook loved garlic, an ingredient that is considered a repellant to Transylvania's most infamous inhabitants, vampires. And while I doubt the inclusion of garlic was meant to banish the undead from the prince's table, the question remains, why are vampires afraid of garlic?

One theory is their association with blood. As far back as Ancient Egypt, the Ebers Papyrus claimed that garlic could be used to ward off snakes, scorpions, and wasps as well as mosquitos and other bloodsucking bugs, and in Ancient Greece and Rome garlic was used to treat all manner of blood diseases. Later, in the medieval era, several diseases were associated with an aversion to garlic and those diseases may have formed the basis for the belief in vampires themselves. Diseases like porphyria. Along with a revulsion to sulfuric foods such as garlic, sufferers of porphyria can have pale skin and form an extreme sensitivity to sunlight. They also exhibit a receding of the lips and gums, giving their teeth a more fang-like appearance.

Even more vampiric is rabies. Also a possible origin for the belief in werewolves, this disease was often spread via the bite of a dog or a bat.

continues

Beef with Garlic Harvester Sauce

continued

Over the next few days, the victim would completely change in demeanor and appearance, becoming more aggressive and violent, culminating in a froth of bloody foam dripping from their mouth. The sufferer's sense of smell would become heightened, making things like certain herbs and garlic repugnant to them. The causes of these diseases being unknown at the time, many attributed the change to demonic possession; thus a bit of garlic could be just the thing you need to save you from harm.

The superstition remained a southeastern European phenomenon until 1897, when the Irish author Bram Stoker included garlic as one of the weapons used against Dracula in his book of the same name. Most of his notions on fighting vampires came from Emily Gerard's 1888 book, *The Land Beyond the Forest: Facts, Figures, and Fancies from Transylvania,* in which she wrote: "In very obstinate cases of vampirism it is recommended to cut off the head, and replace it in the coffin with the mouth filled with garlic." And that is precisely what Dr. Van Helsing does to poor Lucy Westenra after she rises from her coffin, transformed into a vampire by Count Dracula. While few people worry about actual vampires coming through their window today, I say it couldn't hurt to always keep some garlic in the house, if only to make this wonderful beef with garlic harvester sauce.

MAKES 12 SERVINGS   **COOK TIME:** 4 HOURS 15 MINUTES

3½ to 4 pounds (1.75 kg) boneless chuck roast, trussed

2 teaspoons freshly ground black pepper

2 teaspoons kosher salt, divided

2 tablespoons (30 ml) extra-virgin olive oil

2 cups (300 g) finely chopped parsley root or parsnips

1 large onion, finely chopped

½ cup (15 g) torn fresh parsley leaves

3 cups (700 ml) water

1. Preheat the oven to 300°F/150°C.

2. Prepare the roast by rubbing it with pepper and 1 teaspoon of salt. Heat the olive oil in a Dutch oven or large oven-safe pot over medium-high heat. Once the oil is shimmering, brown the roast on all sides, 8 to 10 minutes. Then remove the roast and set it aside on a plate.

3. Add the parsley root or parsnips, onion, parsley leaves, and remaining teaspoon of salt to the pot and cook until the onion is tender and begins to brown, about 8 to 10 minutes. If the vegetables look too dry, add another tablespoon of olive oil. Once the vegetables are cooked, remove as much of them as is easily done and set them aside. It's okay if you don't get everything out of the pot. Deglaze the pot with 3 cups of water, making sure to scrape down any browned bits from the sides of the pot and anything stuck to the bottom.

FOR THE SAUCE:
6 medium eggs at room temperature

⅓ cup (80 ml) white wine vinegar

2 tablespoons peeled and crushed garlic

½ teaspoon freshly ground black pepper

4. Carefully set the roast and its juices back into the pot with the water. Add the vegetables back in and arrange them around the roast. Bring the water to a simmer, then cover the pot and transfer it to the oven to cook for 1 hour per pound. A 3½ pound roast should take about 3½ hours. You'll know the roast is cooked when a fork inserted will twist with little resistance. Remove the pot from the oven and carefully remove the roast and set it on a plate to rest for 15 minutes while you prepare the sauce.

5. Make the sauce: Spoon 1 cup (or as close to it as possible) of the fat and drippings from the pot that the roast was cooked in, set aside. You are likely to get some onion with the drippings, but do not take any of the larger vegetable pieces. Whisk the eggs in a medium saucepan until smooth and then, while continuing to whisk, slowly add the vinegar until incorporated. Add the garlic and pepper and whisk until fully combined. Then, while whisking vigorously, very slowly add the cup of drippings to the eggs. The goal is to temper the eggs, and if you add the hot drippings too quickly the eggs will curdle. Once the drippings are incorporated, set the saucepan over medium-low heat, gently stirring as the sauce begins to thicken to the consistency of heavy cream, about 5 minutes, then serve.

6. Carve the roast into thick slices and serve with the vegetables and a little of the sauce. It can be a strong sauce, so use it sparingly.

Precedella

XXXXXXXXXXXXXXXX

City/Region: Germany
Time Period: 1581

> ### FROM HISTORY
>
> *Take fair flour, a good amount of egg yolk, and a little wine, sugar and anise and make a dough with it. Roll it finely long and round with clean hands and make little pretzels. Set in a warm oven and bake, not burning it but until dried so they are crisp and good. You may or may not use cinnamon. And it is called Precedella.*
>
> —Marx Rumpolt, *Ein New Kochbuch*

The Last Supper, from Bavaria, J. Paul Getty Museum MS Ludwig VII 1, fol. 38

The first origin story of pretzels dates to AD 610, with an Italian monk instructing his pupils in their lenten prayers. In an effort to reward them for a job well done, he gave them a treat: a bit of bread twisted into the shape of a child's arms folded in prayer, and he dubbed them *pretiola*, or "little rewards." A wonderful origin story with almost no truth to it. Unfortunately, nobody really knows where pretzels got their start or their name. The Germans claim that they first twisted bread into knots and called them *bracellus* after the Latin word for "bracelet." Whoever invented them, it is undoubtedly the Germans who made them famous. Their popularity there was such that in 1111 they began to appear on the emblems of bakers' guilds, and in the tenth century they're seen in depictions of the Last Supper in Bavarian churches (e.g., *The Last Supper*, from Bavaria, J. Paul Getty Museum MS Ludwig VII 1, fol. 38).

Just like the apocryphal Italian monk origin story, another story of pretzel-making monks is worth repeating even if it's likely untrue. In 1529, the city of Vienna was under siege by the Ottomans led by Suleiman the Magnificent. He instructed his army to dig tunnels to undermine the walls of the city, but his engineers did not take into account the basement of the monastery. As the monks were baking their pretzels, they heard the scratching of the Ottoman shovels on the other side of the basement wall and quickly raised the alarm. The Imperial Landsknechte were called and they stopped the enemy before their plan could be carried out. In gratitude

continues

Precedella

continued

for saving the city, the Habsburg emperor, Charles V, bestowed upon the monks a coat of arms featuring the pretzel.

Today the pretzel has all but lost its monastic connection, but its popularity is greater than ever, whether the soft, lye-soaked Bavarian pretzel, the buttery Danish Kringler, or *precedella*.

MAKES 8 PRETZELS **COOK TIME:** 40 MINUTES

2½ cups (300 g) all-purpose flour

½ teaspoon ground aniseed

½ teaspoon ground cinnamon (optional or add to taste)

½ teaspoon sea salt

3 large egg yolks

¾ cup (150 g) granulated sugar

⅓ cup (80 ml) sweet white wine

FOR THE EGG WASH:
1 large egg

1 tablespoon water

1. Preheat the oven to 350°F/180°C. Prepare a lined baking sheet.

2. Sift the flour into a medium bowl, then whisk in the aniseed, cinnamon, and salt.

3. In a separate bowl, beat the egg yolks and sugar together until smooth and pale yellow. Then add the wine and mix until smooth. Fold in the flour mixture, one third at a time, making sure it is fully incorporated before the next addition. The dough should be stiff enough to roll into ropes by hand. If it is not, add more flour 1 tablespoon at a time until the dough is the right consistency. Divide the dough into eighths.

4. To shape the pretzels, roll a piece of dough into a long rope about ½ inch (1.25 cm) in width. Take the rope of dough and form a circle. Then take the rope ends and twist the rope together in the middle. Press the ends down on the bottom edge of the circle— if you imagine a clockface, at 7 and 5, respectively. Manipulate the dough until the shape is even, then, using a spatula, transfer onto the lined baking sheet.

5. Once all of the pretzels have been shaped, mix the egg and water together in a small bowl and brush the pretzels with the egg wash. Bake for 12 to 15 minutes, or until they are lightly browned.

Lemonade

City/Region: France
Time Period: 1651

A vendor of lemonade and barley water in Paris is carrying a large drinks container on her back as she walks through the street by Richard Bridgens

Lemonade, as we know it today, is a French invention from around the time of this recipe from *Le cuisinier françois*, one of France's most influential cookbooks of the seventeenth century. Lemonade quickly took off to become a favorite drink of Paris, where it was sold on the streets by the Compagnie de Limonadiers, a lemonade company that formed in 1676. While these roving lemonade merchants provided the citizens of Paris with refreshment, there is also a theory that they spared the city from an outbreak of plague in the late seventeenth century. The disease ravaged much of France at the time, but Paris remained little affected, and it's possible this was due in part to the heaps of lemon peels on the streets left behind by the Compagnie de Limonadiers. The peels contain limonene and linalool, both of which kill the larvae of fleas and are still used in many pet shampoos today, so while this is just a theory, it has some scientific merit to back it up.

While lemonade received no credit for dampening the plague at the time, it was thought to be an excellent drink for the convalescent and is included in lists of medicinal drinks throughout the eighteenth and nineteenth centuries. In 1887, *The Yorkville Enquirer* ran a story featuring the remedial effects of lemonade:

A lady whose husband had a severe cold recommended flaxseed lemonade. "Huh!" he said, irascibly, "a man can't have a cold without everybody suggesting some food remedy. I'll send for a doctor." So the doctor came, charged the sick man $2 for his visit and advised flaxseed lemonade.

It was around this time that lemonade, already popular in the southern United States, gained favor all across the country, not because of its medicinal properties, but because it's not alcoholic, as long as it's not from Long Island. The temperance movement had been fighting the evils of alcohol throughout much of the nineteenth century, but in 1877 it found a champion in the form of the First Lady, Lucy Webb Hayes. Lucy was instrumental in her husband, nineteenth president Rutherford B. Hayes, banning alcohol at all state functions, and one of the replacement beverages was lemonade. In later decades she would be given the nickname "Lemonade Lucy."

As the movement gained political power, the Woman's Christian Temperance Union adopted the slogan "Good-bye to liquor, here's to lemonade," and recipes for the drink began to populate the temperance sections of many cocktail books of the early twentieth century. Though sometimes the recipe would cross over into the more traditional cocktail section, where lemon juice was partially replaced with sherry. While I wouldn't mind trying one of those sherry-laced lemonades, I've decided to opt for a nonalcoholic version in this book, one that could have been enjoyed at the table of Lemonade Lucy.

A narrative study showing a lady in contemplation whilst squeezing a lemon into a glass by Louis-Charles Verwée

MAKES 4 SERVINGS   **COOK TIME:** 10 MINUTES

6 small lemons

2 small oranges

1 cup (200 g) granulated sugar

1 quart (1 liter) water

1. Grate the zest from ½ lemon and ½ orange and set aside. Juice all of the lemons and oranges.

2. In a large pitcher, dissolve the sugar in the water, then stir in the juice from the lemons and oranges and the zest. Set a square of cheesecloth in a second pitcher and strain the lemonade through it. Serve chilled.

Potage d'Onions au Lait (Onion Soup with Milk)

✕✕✕✕✕✕✕✕✕✕✕✕✕✕✕

City/Region: France
Time Period: 1651

FROM HISTORY

After your onion is cut very thin and sautéed in butter until it's well browned, cook it in a little water well seasoned with salt and pepper. After it is done, add milk to it and boil it. Baking your crusts dry, serve it promptly.

—François Pierre de la Varenne, *Le cuisinier français*

The suicide of François Vatel

This onion soup with milk is a simpler precursor to today's French onion soup, something I'll order anytime I see it on a menu. The main differences are that this recipe uses milk instead of stock and is without the iconic melted Gruyère cheese on top, though if you were to add it, I can't imagine anyone minding. The recipe comes from *Le cuisinier français* by François Pierre de la Varenne. It was written during the reign of Louis XIV, a golden age for France and particularly for French cuisine. But even during the reign of the Sun King, there was the occasional cloudy day for French cookery.

It was April 1671 at Château de Chantilly, home of Louis de Bourbon, Prince of Condé. The château was all abuzz, as the prince's cousin Louis XIV himself was coming for the weekend. A stressful visit at any time, as Louis traveled with hundreds of courtiers and thousands of guests, but this visit had the stress dialed up. Only a few years earlier, the prince had been on the losing side of a civil war against his cousin, and while publicly he had been forgiven, there was still tension. The weekend had to go off without a hitch, and the festivities and stress fell upon the prince's maître d'hôtel, François Vatel.

Vatel was no stranger to high-profile guests, including the king. He had served some of France's most powerful people and had gained a reputation for perfection so great that he'd earned what few in his position had before: his own apartments and the great honor of being allowed to carry a sword. The latter being an important fact to keep in mind. Vatel was used to the high-pressure situation he would be in that weekend, though the rocky relationship between the king and his employer no doubt added to his stress.

continues

Potage d'Onions au Lait (Onion Soup with Milk)

continued

Reception of the Grand Condé at Versailles by Jean-Léon Gérôme

According to those who attended the festivities that weekend, the first night was a triumph, though not without its issues. The moon was bright, which was a boon for an evening hunt, but eclipsed the fireworks, which were already obscured by a light fog. The meal, while remarkable, turned out to be short on the roast meat, as more guests had arrived than Vatel had expected. He was heard to have muttered to his employer, "I have lost my honor! I cannot bear this disgrace." The prince assured him that all was well, but it was clear the maître d' was vexed by the evening and the next morning proved to be the boiling point.

It was a Friday, and on Fridays it was forbidden by the Church to eat meat. Vatel had ordered lobster, fish, and other seafood from the ports of Normandy and expected it delivered early that morning, but when it came it was only a fraction of the seafood he'd ordered:

> *"Is this all?" Vatel said. "It is, sir," said the man, not knowing that Vatel had dispatched other people to all the seaports around. Vatel waited for some time; the other purveyors did not arrive; his head grew distracted; he thought there was no more fish to be had. He flew to Gourville, "Sir, I cannot outlive this disgrace." Gourville laughed at him. Vatel, however, went to his apartment, and setting the hilt of his sword against the door, after two ineffectual attempts, succeeded in the third, in forcing his sword through his heart. At that instant the carrier arrived with the fish.*
>
> —*The Letters of Madame de Sévigné to Her Daughter and Friends* (edited by Sarah Josepha Buell Hale, 1869)

A heartbreaking and unthinkable outcome, at least from a modern perspective, but an insight into the importance of being in charge of the meals of seventeenth-century French royalty. So, as you prepare your Potage d'Onions au Lait, appreciate the fact that you can do so under no real pressure, and do spare a thought for poor Monsieur Vatel.

MAKES 4 SERVINGS **COOK TIME:** 1 HOUR 15 MINUTES

2 large yellow onions

4 tablespoons (57 g) salted butter

1½ cups (350 ml) water

Kosher salt

Freshly ground black pepper

3 cups (700 ml) whole milk at room temperature

8 to 12 thin slices of stale French baguette

Olive oil, optional

1. Slice the peeled and trimmed onions down the middle lengthwise, then slice them into very thin strips. Melt the butter in a large saucepan over medium heat. Lower the heat to low and add the onions, cooking them until they are a dark golden brown, about 45 minutes. Stir often to prevent the onions from burning.

2. Once the onions are cooked, pour the water into the saucepan, scraping the sides and bottom with a wooden spoon. Add the salt and pepper to taste. Allow to come to a simmer, cover the saucepan, and simmer for 15 minutes. Add the milk and bring the soup back to a simmer, then raise the heat to a medium temperature and let it come to a gentle boil, watching it closely. Once it starts to boil, remove the soup from the heat.

3. Preheat the oven to 400°F/205°C. Prepare a sheet pan lined with aluminum foil.

4. Arrange the sliced baguette on the sheet pan. (You can lightly brush the baguette with olive oil, but this is not necessary.) Toast the bread on the upper rack of the oven until lightly browned, 5 to 7 minutes. Set the toasts on the bottoms of 4 bowls, then ladle the onion soup on top; alternatively, float the toasts on top of the soup in the bowls. Serve immediately.

Cannetons de Roüen à l'échalote (Rouen Duck with Shallots)

City/Region: France
Time Period: 1739

Louis XV, copy by Jean-Martial Fredou after Louis-Michel van Loo

This dish, perhaps a precursor to the sickly-sweet duck à l'orange so popular in the 1960s, comes from a cookbook written during the reign of Louis XV of France and its recipes could have very well adorned the tables of the monarch himself. It was during his reign that French haute cuisine blossomed:

The reign of Louis XV was no less happy for gastronomy . . . the spirit of conviviality invaded every class of society. It is during this period that there was generally established more orderliness in the meals, more cleanliness and elegance, and those various refinements of service which, having increased steadily until our own time, threaten now to overstep all limits and lead us to the point of ridicule.
—Jean Anthelme Brillat-Savarin, *The Physiology of Taste*[1]

Louis XV toned down the ostentatious court life for which his predecessor, Louis XIV, was so famous. Louis XIV held daily the Grand Couvert, a meal sporting 40 to 170 dishes, which were announced as they paraded past the king while musicians played the latest hits. The entire court of Versailles crowded around as the Sun King tried or else waved away each new dish.

Any food the king and his family did not eat was then sold to the same courtiers who had watched the spectacle. But when Louis XV came to power, he deemed the meal a bit much for his daily supper and so often ate in private, only rolling out the Grand Couvert for special occasions. Though on such occasions the menu, even if toned down from the previous generation, was fit for a king. One supper in September 1755 called for six courses instead of the usual eight, but one course consisted of sixteen dishes, including rabbit, pheasant, quail, turtledove, sweetbreads, veal, and even Rouen duckling just like the one that follows.

MAKES 1 DUCK **COOK TIME:** 2 HOURS 20 MINUTES

1 duck (approximately 5 pounds) (2.2 kg)

2 teaspoons kosher salt

1 quart (1 liter) duck stock

1 tablespoon (15 g) unsalted butter

2 large shallots, minced (approximately ¾ cup)

½ cup (120 ml) freshly squeezed orange juice

1. Wash the duck, inside and out, and dry thoroughly. Rub the outside of the duck with salt, then allow it to rest, uncovered, in the refrigerator for 1 hour or overnight.

2. Preheat the oven to 350°F/175°C.

3. Remove the duck from the refrigerator and score the breast with a knife in a crosshatch pattern. Cut only deep enough to expose the fat without cutting through the fat into the meat. Set the duck on the rack in a roasting pan or on a baking sheet with a cooling rack to lift the duck off the baking sheet. Roast in the oven for 20 minutes per pound or until an instant-read thermometer inserted into the breast reaches 165°F/75°C.

4. Thirty minutes before the duck is ready, prepare the sauce. Add the duck stock to a medium saucepan set over low heat. Without boiling, allow the stock to simmer until it has reduced to ¼ of the original amount (approximately 1 cup/235 ml). While the stock reduces, melt the tablespoon of butter in a small pan over a medium heat. Add the minced shallots to the pan and cook, stirring, until they become translucent, about 5 minutes. Once the stock is reduced, add the cooked shallots and the orange juice to the saucepan and stir to combine. Allow the sauce to come to a simmer and simmer for 5 minutes.

5. When the duck is roasted, remove it from the oven and set on a plate to rest for 10 minutes. Then slice and serve with the shallot and orange sauce.

Semlor (Hettwägg med mandel)

XXXXXXXXXXXXXXXXX

City/Region: Sweden
Time Period: 1755

Frontispiece of *Hjelpreda i hushållningen för unga fruentimber*

FROM HISTORY

Hettwägg med mandel—Take small round wheat bread buns and slice a round plate from the top, then dig out all the insides and put it in a bowl, soak it with sweet cream or milk and mix it well with a spoon; take an egg for each bun and mix in to the wet bread, add to it peeled and fairly finely crushed almonds, sugar, 2 tablespoons of melted butter for each bun and a little salt, stir this well together and put on a fire pot so that nothing solidifies, then fill in the empty buns, and lay the round plate on top, tie well around with thick string, so that the plate remains in place, and put the buns in a wide pot so that they can stand next to each other, then pour milk in the same pot, but not so much that it submerges them, and then let boil for half an hour. . . . In another container boil a "stop" of sweet milk or more, depending on the quantity of the bread, and put in it a little sugar and butter; When it is to be served, the string is removed and the buns are placed in a deep dish, the boiled milk is thickened with two egg yolks, then a little milk is poured on the buns and the rest is poured into a bowl to carry in when eaten.

—Cajsa Warg, *Hjelpreda i hushållningen för unga fruentimber* (translated by Tova Äng)[1]

continues

Semlor (Hettwägg med mandel)

continued

Adolf Fredrik by Lorens Pasch the Younger

Still eaten in Sweden every year on Fat Tuesday, *semlor* (singular *semla*) are soft, sweetened buns, often flavored with cardamom and filled with an almond paste and whipped cream. This recipe, by Cajsa Warg from 1755, is essentially that, but the whipped cream is replaced by boiling the bun and almond filling in warm milk—and this is likely the version that killed King Adolf Frederick of Sweden.

Born in Lübeck, in modern-day Germany, Adolf Frederick was elected to the throne of Sweden in 1743 and was crowned in 1751. He had the good fortune to reign during the time of peace and prosperity known as the Age of Liberty. At the time, the governing of the country was in the hands of the Riksdag of the Estates, a sort of parliament, leaving King Adolf to lead a life of luxury with little responsibility. His biggest headache was keeping the queen, Louisa Ulrika, from overthrowing the government. Louisa attempted this on several occasions, making her a much more interesting historical figure than her husband, who preferred to spend his time crafting snuffboxes and eating, the latter of which killed him.

On February 12, 1771, the King sat down to a meal of lobster, caviar, sauerkraut, and kippers, which he washed down with a bottle of champagne. Then, already stuffed, he indulged in fourteen servings of *hettwägg* or *semlor* in hot milk:

> *After the meal, His Majesty was cheerful, happy and content . . . but at about 8 o'clock in the evening his majesty was attacked rather hastily by a violent stomach cramp. . . . His Majesty sat down on the nearest chair by the door . . . the color of his face changed, and then at once gave up his precious spirit.*
> —Herman Schützercrantz, Archiater to King Adolf Frederick, *The Misfortunes of Swedish Kings*[2]

While it was likely some other gastrointestinal issue that did his royal person in, in Sweden the fourteen servings of *semlor* often gets the credit. So, while you enjoy these, please keep your portion at no more than thirteen.

MAKES 12 *SEMLOR*   **COOK TIME:** 3 HOURS

FOR THE DOUGH:
1¼ cups (295 ml) whole milk

¼ cup (50 g) granulated sugar

4 cups (480 g) bread flour

2¼ teaspoons (7 g) instant yeast

1½ teaspoons kosher salt

1 teaspoon ground cardamom

6 tablespoons (85 g) unsalted butter, softened

2 large eggs, beaten

FOR THE EGG WASH:
1 large egg white

1 tablespoon water

FOR THE FILLING:
1 cup (235 ml) heavy whipping cream

6 large eggs, beaten

2 cups (260 g) coarsely ground raw, unsalted almonds

1 cup (226 g) salted butter, melted

½ cup (100 g) granulated sugar

1 teaspoon kosher salt

FOR BOILING:
1 quart (1 liter) whole milk for boiling

FOR THE SWEET MILK:
1 quart (1 liter) whole milk

½ cup (100 g) granulated sugar

4 tablespoons (56 g) salted butter

2 large egg yolks at room temperature

1. Make the dough: Warm the milk in a small saucepan over medium heat to 100°F/38°C. Stir the sugar into the milk until dissolved. In a large bowl, whisk together the flour, yeast, salt, and cardamom. Pour the milk mixture into the flour mixture and work it together into a ragged dough. Add the softened butter and the eggs and work to combine. Knead the dough until it becomes a smooth but sticky ball. Then place the dough in a lightly oiled bowl, cover, and let rise for between 60 and 90 minutes, or until it's doubled in size.

2. Once the dough has risen, punch the air out and turn it out onto a lightly floured surface. Divide it into 12 equal portions, then shape them into buns. Set them on two lined baking sheets. Lightly cover the buns and allow to rise for another 45 minutes.

3. Preheat the oven to 400°F/200°C.

4. Once the buns have risen, make the egg wash: Whisk the egg white and water in a small bowl. Brush it over the tops of the buns. Then, one tray at a time, bake the buns for 15 minutes. Set the baked buns on a cooling rack to cool completely.

5. Make the filling: Once the buns have cooled, slice the top off about ¼ of the way down the bun. Set the tops aside and dig out the inside crumb of the bun, making sure not to create any holes in it, as you would for a bread bowl. Set the buns aside with their matching tops. Tear the scooped-out bread into small pieces about the size of a thumbnail and put the bread in a large pot. Pour the heavy whipping cream over the bread and mix to allow it to soak up as much cream as possible, then add the beaten eggs, ground almonds, melted butter, sugar, and salt and mix until combined. Set the pot over low heat and, stirring continuously, cook until the egg is cooked and the mixture begins to darken slightly, about 5 minutes. Remove the pot from the heat and divide the filling into 12 portions. Fill the scooped-out buns, then set their tops back on.

continues

Semlor (Hettwägg med mandel)

continued

6. Take a foot of kitchen string and wrap it under the bottom of a bun, tying a bow at the top as if to hold down the lid. Make sure you can use the bow to easily lift the bun, as it will make it easier to remove from the pot after cooking. Repeat on all the other buns.

7. Set a trivet or upside-down plate on the bottom of the largest pot you can find. This is to prevent the buns from sticking to the bottom as they cook. Then place several of the buns on the trivet in the pot, leaving them enough space so they do not touch each other. Carefully pour enough milk into the pot so that it reaches about halfway up the sides of the buns, then set over medium-high heat and bring to a boil. Boil for 30 minutes while you prepare the sweetened milk.

8. Prepare the sweet milk: In a medium saucepan set over medium heat, whisk together the milk and sugar and bring to a simmer. Whisk in the butter until melted, then, while whisking, add the egg yolks. Gently stir as it simmers. It should thicken slightly after several minutes—note that it will not thicken as much as a custard. Lower the heat to keep the sweet milk warm while the buns finish boiling.

9. Once the buns are cooked, use the string and a spatula to remove them from the pot and set them in a serving dish. Remove the string and pour a bit of the sweet milk around the buns, then serve.

Cook's Notes: If you wish to have more modern-style *semlor*, fill the buns with half the amount of almond filling, then fill the rest with whipped cream and set the lid on top and sprinkle with powdered sugar. Skip the steps of boiling in milk and making the sweet milk and go straight to eating.

The original recipe calls for a "stop" of milk, an old unit of measurement that was about 1.3 liters.

Pomodori Farciti all'Erbette

City/Region: Italy
Time Period: 1773

Vincenzo Corrado

Tomatoes are a New World food, a favorite of the civilizations of Mesoamerica since at least AD 700. The Aztecs called them *tomatl*, and when the Spanish arrived in the 1500s they took the fruit and the name, as best they could pronounce it, back to Europe with them. But tomatoes got a mixed reception. Some dubbed it the apple of gold or *pom d'or*, from which the Italians got *pomodoro*, and believed it to be an aphrodisiac. But others equated tomatoes with their cousin belladonna or deadly nightshade, a favorite poison of sixteenth-century Italy, and the fear seemed to be borne out when tomatoes began poisoning people. Or at least people thought they were. More likely, it was the acidic tomato leaching lead out of the pewter plates that the wealthy of the sixteenth and seventeenth centuries used. But the poor, who couldn't afford pewter, seemed unaffected and tomatoes began to find their way into the everyday cuisine of the Mediterranean.

Farther north, in England, and across the Atlantic in the American colonies, tomatoes were all the rage, but mostly as decoration, adding color to gardens when flowers weren't enough. Even by the early nineteenth century, while the southern states began to feature tomatoes on their tables, in the North their culinary use was still underappreciated:

> *Hardly two persons in a hundred, on first tasting it, thought that they would ever be induced to taste that sour trash a second time.*
> —J. B. Garber (Pennsylvania, c. 1820)

Eventually, the French influence on southern cuisine spread the use of the tomato throughout the United States, and at the end of the nineteenth

continues

Pomodori Farciti all'Erbette

continued

century an influx of immigrants from Italy made the fruit essential to any diet. But is the tomato a fruit? Any good botanist would say yes, but the United States Supreme Court would beg to differ, though perhaps not for the reason you might think.

The Tariff of 1883 required a tax to be paid on any imported vegetables, but fruit was exempt, so when a tariff was imposed on a shipment of Caribbean tomatoes destined for John Nix & Co. of New York, Mr. Nix filed a lawsuit, since tomatoes were a fruit. The case made its way to the Supreme Court, and in 1893, in the case of *Nix v. Hedden*, Justice Horace wrote an opinion stating: "Botanically speaking, tomatoes are the fruit of a vine, just as are cucumbers, squashes, beans, and peas. But in the common language of the people, whether sellers or consumers of provisions, all these are vegetables."

And in the words of the humorist Miles Kington: "Knowledge is knowing a tomato is a fruit; wisdom is not putting it in a fruit salad."[2] I think we're safe frying it with a mix of herbs and cheese.

MAKES 6 TO 8 SERVINGS **COOK TIME:** 30 MINUTES

½ cup finely chopped fresh Italian parsley

½ cup finely chopped yellow or white onion

¼ cup finely chopped fresh sorrel (or substitute arugula or spinach with a squeeze of lemon)

2 tablespoons finely chopped fresh mint

4 ounces (113g) prosciutto

Salt

Freshly ground black pepper

8 ounces (226 g) Provatura cheese (or fresh mozzarella)

3 large egg yolks

6 to 8 medium fresh tomatoes

2 or 3 tablespoons extra-virgin olive oil

Ham broth or crusty bread, if desired, for serving

1. Preheat the oven to 350°F/175°C.

2. Mix the parsley, onion, sorrel, and mint together in a medium bowl. Tear the prosciutto into small pieces, then mix into the herbs and add salt and pepper to taste. Grate the cheese into the mixture, then add the egg yolks and mix together to form a paste.

3. Slice off the tops of the tomatoes and scoop out the inside with a spoon, discarding the tops and insides of the tomatoes. Stuff the hollow tomatoes with the herb mixture until full but not packed too tightly. The filling should be flush with the top of the tomato.

4. Add enough olive oil to cover the bottom of an oven-safe frying pan and set over medium heat. Pan-fry the tomatoes, bottom down, for 2 to 3 minutes, then use tongs to quickly flip them over and to prevent the filling from falling out. Pan-fry top down for 2 to 3 minutes. Then place the frying pan into the oven and bake for 10 minutes. Remove the pan from the oven and serve hot. The original recipe says these can be served with a ham broth, but I find they're best served with a bit of crusty Italian bread, if desired.

Cook's Note: The quantities of the herbs and onion can be modified to suit your preference.

La Pêche Melba

✕✕✕✕✕✕✕✕✕✕✕✕✕✕✕

City/Region: France/England
Time Period: 1903

FROM HISTORY

Peach Melba. Poached in vanilla syrup, placed on a layer of vanilla ice cream and topped with raspberry purée.

—Auguste Escoffier, *Le guide culinaire*

Nellie Melba

When placing the recipe for La Pêche Melba or Peach Melba in this book, I had trouble deciding if it belonged with the English recipes or the other European recipes. It's definite that it was first made at the Savoy Hotel in London, England, but the creator, Auguste Escoffier, is so undeniably French that including it in the English section seemed an injustice, so here we are. Peach Melba was named after the late-nineteenth-century Australian operatic soprano Nellie Melba (of Melba toast fame) and is but one of the many dishes Chef Escoffier named after one of his many famous patrons.

Auguste Escoffier cut his teeth back in France, where he served as military chef during the Franco-Prussian War, first to the field marshals of the French army and then his fellow POWs during a six-month stint at Wiesbaden. After the war, he returned to Paris to cook at Le Petit Moulin Rouge, opened his own restaurant, Le Faisan d'Or, in Cannes, and eventually found a position at the Grand Hotel National in Lucerne, where he met an ambitious hotel manager named César Ritz. Their partnership would become one of the most famous in culinary history, and in 1890 Richard D'Oyly Carte, famed producer of the operettas of Gilbert and Sullivan, invited the duo to London to take control of his Savoy Hotel.

It was at the Savoy that Escoffier became a household name as he wooed the London elite with an ever-evolving menu and personalized dishes for the likes of Nellie Melba, the actress Sarah Bernhardt, and even the Prince of Wales. It was there that Escoffier also perfected a new method of managing a hotel kitchen called *La Brigade de Cuisine* or "The Kitchen Brigade." Before the introduction of the brigade, each cook would be in charge of a different dish, all of those dishes coming together only at the end to form a meal. But Escoffier set his kitchen up based on military hierarchy, placing

continues

La Pêche Melba

continued

The London Savoy Hotel
Restaurant c. 1900

himself as field marshal and below him an army of cooks each with an individual task. Someone in charge of only sauces, another who only cooked fish, and another who only roasted meat. Dozens of positions where his cooks could perfect a single task, each contributing to part of a dish that would come together under his watchful eye. It was the culinary precursor to Henry Ford's assembly line and was so successful that most restaurants today still follow a version of *La Brigade de Cuisine*.

Escoffier and Ritz eventually left the Savoy, which, at the time, was said to be for personal reasons. Recent documents have revealed accusations of bribery and embezzlement were the real reason for the departure, but leaving the Savoy was perhaps the best thing to happen to both of their careers. César Ritz founded the Ritz Hotel with Auguste Escoffier as the head of the restaurant and together they built a chain of hotels the name of which became synonymous with style and opulence, and while it was Ritz's name that most remember, it's Escoffier's contribution to the partnership from which we all benefit today, every time we eat in a restaurant.[1]

6 ripe peaches

1 tablespoon granulated sugar

2 cups (250 g) ripe raspberries

1¼ cup (150 g) powdered sugar

2 pints (1 liter) French vanilla ice cream

Raw almond slivers, for garnish

1. Bring a large pot of water to a boil on the stove. While it heats, prepare a large, wide bowl of ice water and set aside. Two at a time, place the peaches in the boiling water for 7 seconds, using tongs to turn them after a few seconds, then remove them and plunge them into the ice water. Leave them there for 10 seconds, then remove them and set on a plate. Once all 6 peaches are blanched, remove the peel; it should slough off easily. Then, using a very sharp knife, slice the peaches in half and remove the pits. Sprinkle each side of each half with granulated sugar and set the peaches on a plate, cover with plastic wrap, and set them in the refrigerator for 1 hour while you make the raspberry sauce.

2. Wash the raspberries, then put them in a blender and puree. Put the puree in a fine-mesh sieve and press it into a medium bowl. It should be smooth and have no seeds. Sift in the powdered sugar and whisk until fully incorporated. Cover the bowl and set it in the refrigerator to chill. Set six dishes in the freezer to chill. It's best if these are metal, but ceramic will work as well.

3. Once everything has chilled, remove the dishes from the freezer and add 2 or 3 large scoops of vanilla ice cream. Place two sugared peach halves on top, then drizzle with the raspberry puree, covering the peaches. Top with almond slivers and serve.

The
NEAR &
FAR EAST

✕✕✕✕

Payasam

City/Region: India
Time Period: c. 12th century

P*ayasam* is the Indian version of rice pudding, though even today it has variants throughout the country such as *kheer, phirni,* or *payesh*. They are made with different rice, different textures, and different flavorings and there is debate as to which was the original version in India. While I'm not going to take a side in the debate, when it comes to the oldest recipe I'm fairly confident this one is it. It was written for Someswara III, a twelfth-century ruler of the Western Chalukya Empire in southern India. Though the history, or rather myth, of *payasam* goes back even before him.

At some point in the murky mists of time, Lord Krishna decided that he was running low on rice. The god took the form of an old sage and went to the court of the king who ruled the region around the Ambalappuzha Temple in Kerala, India. He challenged the king to a game of chaturanga, the ancestor of chess. After much success on the battlefield, the old king fancied himself quite the strategist and agreed to play. He was so confident in his skills that he promised the old man whatever he wished should he win. Krishna thought a moment, then asked only for some grains of rice, the number of which would be based on the game board. One grain for the first square, two grains for the second, four for the third, eight for the fourth, sixteen for the fifth square, and so on. The king, thinking the old man was out of his mind but happy to be getting away with something, agreed. To no surprise, Krishna, a god, won and asked for his reward, which, due to the miracle of exponential growth, was over nine quintillion grains of rice, more than the number of grains of sand on the planet. Seeing the king's expression of despair when the amount of rice was revealed, Lord Krishna took pity on him and told him that he could pay the debt over time. A long time. To this day, the debt is still being paid via a massive bowl of *payasam*

continues

Payasam

continued

served at the Ambalappuzha Temple each day, and Lord Guruvayoorappan, one of Krishna's many forms, accepts his payment.

The moral is twofold: Do your math before agreeing to any deal, and never play board games with a god or else you may need a lot more *payasam* than the few bowls this recipe makes.

MAKES 6 TO 8 SERVINGS   **COOK TIME:** 1 HOUR

1 heaping ½ cup (100 g) dry white rice

1 quart (1 liter) whole milk

1 cup (150 g) grated jaggery (see page 13) or ⅓ cup (67 g) sugar plus 2 tablespoons molasses

¾ teaspoon ground cardamom

10 to 12 threads of saffron

¼ teaspoon kosher salt

1. Rinse the rice well, then put it in a bowl and soak in clean water for 30 minutes, then drain.

2. Pour the milk into a medium saucepan and bring to a boil over medium-high heat. Once the milk is boiling, reduce heat to medium low and add in the drained rice. Allow to boil for 20 minutes or until the rice is soft enough that a grain can be easily mashed between your fingers. Stir every few minutes so the rice does not burn to the bottom of the saucepan.

3. Once the rice is cooked, add the jaggery or sugar, cardamom, saffron (there is no need to grind them), and the salt and mix until incorporated. Allow to simmer for 5 minutes, stirring every minute. Remove the pot from the heat and allow to cool for several minutes. The *payasam* will continue to thicken as it cools. Serve warm or chilled.

Samosas

City/Region: Mughal Empire
Time Period: c. 1590

FROM HISTORY

*Qutáb, which the people of Hindustan
call sanbusah: This is made in several ways.
10 seer meat; 4 s. fine flour; 2 s. g'hi;
1 s. onions; ¼ s. fresh ginger; ½ s. salt;
2 dams pepper and coriander seed; cardamum,
cuminseed, cloves, 1 d. of each; ¼ s. of
summaq. This can be cooked in twenty different
ways, and gives four full dishes.*

—Abu'l-Fazl 'Allami, *A'in-i Akbari*

A page from the medieval
Indian manuscript
*Nimatnama-i-Nasiruddin-
Shahi* (c. 1500)

Samosa, *sanbusah*, *sambusa*, *samusa*, or, in the case of this recipe, Qutáb. Many names for the same thing: pastry stuffed with spiced filling, then baked or fried. It seems like every culture has some form of this dish and, no doubt, many were developed independently from others (I'm looking at you, Chinese steamed dumplings), but for the most part, they all come from one original dish.

Likely made somewhere in Central Asia, the original samosa was a way to preserve meat for long journeys. As Muslim traders traveled across Asia and Africa and into Spain, they brought the samosa with them, and while each culture who adopted the dish made it their own, different shapes, fillings, doughs, and cooking methods, their names are all related. But as diverse as they are, when I hear "samosa" I think India, and that's where the recipe here comes from. It was written around 1590 by Abu'l-Fazl, the historian at the court of Akbar, the greatest of the Mughal emperors, as part of the *A'in-i Akbari*, or *The Administration of Akbar*. Written in Persian, the language of the imperial court, it's a comprehensive five-volume work covering every facet of the emperor's domain from the military, the local tribes within the empire, and religion to morals, sayings of the day, and even a couple pages devoted to the food eaten at the imperial court.

The recipes are lists of ingredients with specific quantities but no direction on how to cook them. In the case of the Qutáb, he says there are

continues

Samosas

continued

twenty different ways to cook them, none of which he describes, so if we are to re-create the Qutáb of the Mughal Empire, we must look to more modern methods of samosa making. Though when it comes to the question of baking versus frying, we have the good fortune to have an actual image of samosa making from the time. It's in another contemporary manuscript, *The Book of Delicacies of Nasir-ud-Din Shah*, and shows samosas being fried in a pan, so that is what we'll be doing here.

MAKES 12 SAMOSAS   **COOK TIME:** 90 MINUTES

FOR THE FILLING:

2 tablespoons (25 g) ghee

1 large onion, finely chopped

2 teaspoons kosher salt, divided

1 pound (450 g) lean ground meat (lamb, beef, or venison)

1 tablespoon (12 g) minced fresh ginger

2 teaspoons ground sumac

1 teaspoon freshly ground black pepper

1 teaspoon ground coriander seed

½ teaspoon ground cardamom

½ teaspoon ground cumin

½ teaspoon ground cloves

Vegetable oil such as soybean or sunflower oil, for frying

FOR THE DOUGH:

4 cups (480 g) cups all-purpose flour

1 teaspoon kosher salt

½ cup (100 g) ghee, melted

½ cup (120 ml) water

Chutney, if desired, for serving

1. Make the filling: Melt 2 tablespoons of ghee over medium heat in a medium skillet. Add the onion and season with 1 teaspoon of salt. Cook until well browned, about 8 minutes, then raise the heat to high and stir in the ground meat and ginger. Season with the remaining 1 teaspoon of salt, sumac, black pepper, coriander, cardamom, cumin, and cloves. Cook, stirring occasionally, until the meat is well done, 8 to 10 minutes. The filling should be quite dry to make it easier to fill the samosas. Break up the meat as small as possible, and once it is cooked remove it from the heat to cool completely while you prepare the dough.

2. Make the dough: Whisk the flour and salt in a large bowl, then pour the ghee into the flour and mix it together using a spoon. Then rub the flour between your palms to further incorporate the ghee, for 2 to 3 minutes. Add the water and begin to form the dough into a ball, adding more water if necessary. Knead the dough on an un-floured surface for about 10 minutes or until it's nice and smooth. Set the dough in a bowl, cover with a damp cloth, and let it rest for 25 minutes.

3. Once the dough has rested, turn it out onto the un-floured surface and knead until it's stiff, 3 to 4 more minutes, then divide it into 6 equal pieces and put all but 1 back in the bowl under the damp cloth. Lightly oil the counter or board and roll the piece of dough into a wide oval, about 8 by 6 inches or a little larger. While you don't want the dough too thick, if it gets too thin it will become hard to shape the samosas. Cut the dough in half crosswise.

continues

Samosas

continued

4. Dip your fingers in a bowl of water, then lightly wet all around the curved edges of one of the two pieces of dough on one side, then wrap it gently around your fingers to form a cone with the flat edge as the opening. Lightly press the edges together to make sure the cone keeps its shape. Then fill the cone with a spoonful of the filling about three-quarters full. Moisten the opening of the cone with water and press it shut, folding the seal over and flattening the side so the samosa can stand up like a pyramid. Set it on a plate and repeat the process until all of the samosas are made. Cover the plate of samosas with a damp towel and set it in the refrigerator for 10 minutes.

5. While the samosas chill, heat a medium saucepan with cooking oil about 3 inches deep to 350°F/175°C. Try to keep the temperature within 15 degrees of this throughout the frying process until the very end. Once the oil reaches the correct temperature, take the samosas out of the refrigerator and carefully set them in it. You should have tiny bubbles rising from the samosas and not hear any sizzling noise. Add as many as you can comfortably fit in the saucepan. Leave them undisturbed for 2 to 3 minutes, at which point they should begin to float. Gently stir them around the oil occasionally so they fry evenly. After 10 to 12 minutes, or when they begin to brown, raise the heat to medium high and let the samosas cook until lightly golden. Then remove them from the oil and set them on a plate lined with paper towel to drain. Serve alone or with chutney, if desired.

Saag

XXXXXXXXXXXXXX

City/Region: Mughal Empire
Time Period: c. 1590

Babur

This recipe for saag, now a staple of Indian cuisine, is from the Mughal Empire, which spanned much of India and Pakistan in the sixteenth, seventeenth, and eighteenth centuries. The empire was founded in 1526 by Babur, "The Tiger," a ruthless conqueror known for his love of food.

Before he died, Babur composed his memoirs, the *Baburnama*, and while he discusses his travels and conquests, he peppers in plenty of discussion of his favorite foods. He starts the work by describing his hometown, Adijān, in modern Uzbekistan:

It produces much grain, fruits in abundance, excellent grapes and melons. . . . Better than the Adijān nashpati melon, there is none . . . and its pheasants grow so surprisingly fat that rumour has it that four people could not finish one they were eating with its stew. . . . Its apricots and pomegranates are most excellent. One sort of pomegranate, they call the Great Seed; its sweetness has a little of the pleasant flavor of the small apricot and it may be thought better than the Semnan pomegranate.

As he travels through Uzbekistan and down into Afghanistan to conquer Kabul, he is always talking of the melons and fruits of the area, often comparing them to those of his youth. He also talks of the country's wine. Babur was a great fan of wine, though he spent much of his life conflicted

Illustration from the *Baburnama* showing Babur visiting a Hindu cave near Bagram

about the drink. He believed his Islamic faith forbade him to drink it, yet threw wild, wine-fueled parties for his men where he loved to sing drinking songs. "Drink wine in the castle of Kabul and send the cup round without pause!" And even when he finally gave up wine completely, he still found himself attending the wine parties of others:

> *There was a wine-party once I went to and . . . at that time I drank no wine. The party was elegant; every sort of wine was set out, with kebabs of fowl and goose, and all sorts of food. . . . I was at two or three of this host's wine-parties . . . but once it was known I did not drink, no pressure to do so was put on me.*

Without wine, Babur turned all of his attention to fruit. After invading Hindustan (modern-day Pakistan and India) he lamented the complete lack of good cuisine and fruit. The only fruits that he thought decent were plantains, as the peel was easily removed, and mangoes:

> *Mangoes, when good, are very good, but, as many as are eaten, few are first-rate. . . . They do make excellent condiments and are also good preserved in syrup. All in all, the mango is the best fruit of Hindustan.*

Alas, there were those who would use his love of food against him. Not long after his bloody conquest of Hindustan, there was an attempt by his Hindustani cooks to poison him:

> *On Friday . . . I ate a dish of hare and fried carrot, took a few mouthfuls of the poisoned food without noticing any unpleasant flavour. . . . Then I felt sick . . . after retching two or three times I . . . vomited. I became suspicious.*

The conqueror brought in a dog who ate some of the ruler's vomit and it, too, became ill. The cook was summoned and tortured before implicating himself, a food taster, two young women, and one old woman as members of the conspiracy. This was Babur's opportunity to show himself as a lenient and forgiving ruler over his new subjects . . . he did not accept the opportunity:

continues

Saag

continued

The taster I had cut in pieces, the cook skinned alive; one of the women I had thrown under an elephant, the other shot with a match-lock. The old woman I had kept under guard; she will meet her doom, the captive of her own act.

As you make this sixteenth-century recipe for Saag, as it might have been eaten by Babur himself, be glad that he's dead and you are in no danger of being skinned alive or squashed by an elephant.

MAKES 4 SERVINGS   **COOK TIME:** 35 MINUTES

10 cups (300 g) spinach leaves and/or other greens

1 cup (90 g) fennel bulb

3-inch piece (20 g) fresh ginger

4 tablespoons (50 g) ghee

⅔ cup (35 g) finely chopped onion

Pinch of kosher salt

½ cup (120 ml) water

½ teaspoon freshly ground black pepper

Pinch of ground cardamom

Pinch of ground cloves

1. Wash and finely mince the spinach and/or other greens and fennel. This can be easily done in batches with a few pulses in a food processor.

2. Wash and peel the ginger, then mince.

3. Melt the ghee in a large skillet over medium-low heat, then add the chopped onion and season with salt. Cook, stirring occasionally, until the onion is soft but not browned, about 5 minutes. Add the ginger and cook for another 2 minutes.

4. Add the greens and fennel and ½ cup of water, then sprinkle with pepper, cardamom, and cloves. Increase the heat to medium and cook, stirring occasionally, until the greens are soft and most of the water has steamed off, 15 to 20 minutes. Once the greens are to your liking, transfer to a bowl and serve immediately.

Niangao

⋊⋉⋊⋉⋊⋉⋊⋉⋊⋉⋊⋉⋊

City/Region: China
Time Period: 544

FROM HISTORY

Ground glutinous rice into flour and sift through fine silk mesh. Mix with water and honey and form into stiff cakes. Use hands to shape cakes to around one foot in length, two inches in width. Cover with the flesh of jujubes and chestnuts and wrap in oiled bamboo leaves. Steam until soft and well cooked.

—Jia Sixie, *Qímín yàoshù* (translated by Roy Chan)[1]

The Chinese dessert Niangao is a dish with an ancient history. Of course, like much ancient history, a bit of myth often creeps in and it's nigh impossible to distinguish between what actually happened and what didn't—but that doesn't make the story any less interesting.

In the fifth century BCE, during a time known as the Spring and Autumn period, in the state of Chu, there was a young man named Wu Zixu. Wu's father did something to anger the king, Ping, though what it was we do not know, nor is it relevant to the story. What matters is that King Ping was so angry that he killed Wu Zixu's father and brother and tried to kill Wu Zixu as well, but Zixu ran before he could be captured. Eventually, the king's men caught up with Wu Zixu, but the stress of running had aged him so much as to make him unrecognizable, a good argument to give the next time someone asks you to run for any reason. I do think it's safe to say that this part of the story can be consigned to the realm of myth. Whatever the true reason, Wu Zixu kept moving along until he reached the neighboring kingdom of Wu.

Wu Zixu devised a long, overly complicated plan to avenge his father and brother, the intricacies of which are lost to history, but what is known is that he went to the Prince of Wu with a plan: murder the prince's uncle, the current King of Wu, so that the prince could be installed as the new ruler. Needing little persuading, the prince led a coup against his uncle and became King Helü of Wu and made Wu Zixu one of his top generals alongside the famed general Sun Tzu.

continues

Niangao

continued

Wu Zixu's escape by
Yoshitoshi

With his newfound military power, Wu Zixu convinced the new king to let him lead an army against his homeland of Chu, which he did, only to find that King Ping had died, leaving his son Zhao as heir. But Wu Zixu felt that one king was as good as another and attacked the capital of Ying anyway, seizing the city and forcing King Zhao to flee. Still sour about his father and brother, Wu Zixu opened the burial mound of King Ping and flogged his corpse three hundred times. With the old king dead, the new king having fled, and Wu Zixu's boss, King Helü, back in the kingdom of Wu, Wu Zixu became de facto ruler of the state of Chu and built mighty walls around the capital city. Everything was going Wu Zixu's way until his boss and champion, King Helü, died and left his son, Fuchai, on the throne.

Fuchai had a new adviser who didn't much care for Wu Zixu and poured poison into the new king's ear. When Wu Zixu warned King Fuchai of an impending attack from a neighboring kingdom, he rebuffed the warning and went so far as to give Wu Zixu a sword, commanding him to commit suicide, a recurring theme in Chinese history. Wu Zixu did as his king commanded, but before he did he told Fuchai's personal guard if the city was ever under siege and its people were starving, to dig at the base of the great city walls, which he'd had built. Only then did Wu Zixu plunge the sword into his belly. Well, it wasn't long before the enemy that he'd warned the king about came-a knockin' on the city gates. The city was under siege, and in no time the people were starving. When they dug at the base of the walls, they found that many of the foundational bricks were not bricks at all but blocks of glutinous rice cakes—Niangao.

Today Niangao is most associated with the Chinese New Year and is made as a round cake, but this recipe, from AD 544, calls for the cake to be formed into the same brick shape that Wu Zixu made his wall from a millennium earlier.

8 to 10 large bamboo leaves (or parchment)

3 tablespoons rice oil or vegetable oil

1 pound (450 g) glutinous rice flour

1 cup (235 ml) water

1 cup (235 ml) honey

8 to 10 dried jujubes, chopped

6 to 8 roasted chestnuts, chopped

1. Place the bamboo leaves in a large pot and set a weight, such as a plate, on top of them. Then cover with cool water and allow to soak overnight, at least 8 hours. (Skip this step if using parchment paper.)

2. Once the leaves are well soaked, pat them dry with a towel, then lightly coat them or the parchment paper with the oil. Line the bottom and sides of a 9-inch loaf pan with the oil-coated leaves or parchment, with several inches of leaf hanging over the edges of the pan.

3. To make the cake, mix the rice flour with the water and honey until they form a dough. Turn it out onto the counter and form it into a brick. The modern version of this dough is a pourable liquid, but this version should be very stiff and easily moldable by hand. Set the brick into the prepared loaf pan and decorate the top with the chopped jujubes and chestnuts. Wrap the leaves around the cake, tucking them into the sides of the pan. If there is any dough showing, set a few leaves over the top of the pan to keep water from dripping into it.

4. Fill a large steamer with water to just below the steaming tray. Heat the water to boiling and set the pan with the cake in and cover, letting it steam for 1½ to 2 hours. Check on the water level periodically to determine if you need to add more boiling water. There should always be plenty but not so much that it touches the bottom of the pan.

5. Once the cake is cooked, remove it from the steamer and let it cool completely, still wrapped in the bamboo leaves or parchment. Once it is cooled, remove the Niangao from the pan and peel back the leaves. The cake should look like a brick. It is served best sliced thin and fried in a skillet with a little oil or an egg.

Yuanxiao

City/Region: Ming China
Time Period: 1620s

> ## FROM HISTORY
>
> *The cooking method uses glutinous rice that has been ground into a fine powder. Inside the wrapper the filling comprises the flesh of walnuts and white sugar. Water is sprinkled on the filling and the balls are rolled around in flour to form them. They are as big as walnuts. This is the same as what the people of the Jiangnan region call tangyuan.*
>
> —Liu Ruoyu, *Zhuo zhong zhi* (translated by Roy Chan)[1]

Yuanxiao is a ball of glutinous rice stuffed with a sweet walnut filling, but it's the source of this seventeenth-century recipe, the *Zhuo zhong zhi* by Liu Ruoyu, that has a story worth telling.

The Ming court, under the teenage Tianqi Emperor, was run by a powerful and scheming eunuch named Wei Zhongxian. Powerful and scheming eunuchs were actually quite the trend in Imperial China, but none were as formidable as Wei. He, along with the emperor's nurse, Madame Ke, removed all others who held power over the emperor. Some were banished, some starved to death, and others were forced to commit suicide. The pair kept the young emperor ignorant of the goings-on in his empire while they ran the government.

During Wei's reign of terror, a young eunuch named Liu distinguished himself as an excellent calligrapher, an uncommon skill among the eunuchs of the Forbidden City. His work caught the jealous eye of the illiterate Wei Zhongxian, who, unfriendly to any he believed smart enough to challenge his power, demoted the young scribe to work in the stables. Liu toiled there for several years and added the moniker Ruoyu, which meant "the dumb," to his name to remind himself that feigning stupidity might serve him better in the Wei regime.

But the powerful eunuch eventually found a use for Liu Ruoyu's talent: forgery. Wei had procured a number of blank documents already stamped with the emperor's seal. All he required to govern with impunity was for someone to fill the documents with whatever decrees he wished. Liu was just the man for the job.

The scheme did not last long, though, for when the Tianqi Emperor died at the age of twenty-one his younger brother, Zhu Youjian, came to power as the Chongzhen Emperor. Though only sixteen, Zhu had not yet fallen under Wei Zhongxian's influence, and the new emperor banished the troublesome eunuch, executed Madame Ke, and imprisoned any who had helped Wei, including Liu Ruoyu. While in prison, Liu wrote the *Zhuo zhong zhi*, part protestation of his innocence and part treatise on daily life in the Forbidden City. His writings included a number of recipes, such as this one for Yuanxiao.

Yuanxiao are eaten each year during the Spring Lantern Festival in China, also confusingly known as Yuanxiao.

MAKES 16 YUANXIAO   **COOK TIME:** 2 HOURS 15 MINUTES

1¼ cups (140 g) whole shelled, raw, unsalted walnuts

½ cup (100 g) granulated sugar

4 tablespoons (57 g) unsalted butter, melted

2 cups (225 g) glutinous rice flour (sweet rice flour)

1. Heat a large skillet over medium-high heat. Add the walnuts to the pan in a single layer. Heat them, stirring frequently, until lightly browned, about 5 minutes. Once the walnuts are toasted, remove them from the pan and set aside on a plate to cool, about 10 minutes. Once they are cool, crush the walnuts by hand or in a food processor, until they become almost a coarse flour.

2. Mix the crushed walnuts, sugar, and butter in a bowl until combined. Chill the mixture in the refrigerator for 1 hour.

3. Remove the mixture from the refrigerator and divide it into 16 portions. Using clean hands, roll each portion into a ball and set aside.

4. Fill a large bowl three-quarters full with cold water. In another large bowl, add the glutinous rice flour. Working in batches of 3 or 4 balls at a time, roll the balls in the flour until covered. Put the balls in a fine-mesh strainer. Dip the strainer with the balls briefly in the water, then return to the flour and roll again, coating completely. Repeat this process 7 to 10 times, or until there is no visible filling. Repeat the process until all the balls are coated. Note that cracks

continues

Yuanxiao

continued

may appear in the coating, but as long as the filling is not visible, that is okay.

5. Fill a large pot half-full of water and set it over high heat. Bring the water to a boil. Working in batches, boil 3 or 4 balls until they float to the top, 2 to 3 minutes. Note that the balls will expand, so leave plenty of room in the pot. Once the balls have floated to the top, add a cup of cold water. The balls should sink a bit. Adding cold water will stop the boiling and allow a skin to form on the balls. Allow the water to return to a boil and wait until the balls float again. Remove the balls and set aside. Bring the water back to a boil and repeat the steps with the remaining balls until finished. Serve warm.

Chinese eunuchs from the tomb of Prince Zhanhuai (c. 706)

Nyumen

City/Region: Japan
Time Period: 1643

Orihime and Hikoboshi
by Tsukioka Yoshitoshi

FROM HISTORY

Simmered Noodles
To start with, cut short pieces of somen, boil,
gently dry and put it aside. Add dashi to taremiso,
and when it is steaming, put in the noodles. Add
such things as young mustard greens, nebuka,
and eggplant. It is also served with usumiso.
Add black pepper and sansho powder.

—*Ryori Monogatari* (translated by Joshua Badgley)[1]

Japan is famous for their noodles. Udon, soba, and of course ramen. But this recipe features perhaps the least known but the most delicate and longest of the noodles: *somen*. As far back as 1270, descriptions of *somen* noodles liken them to ropes of wheat and call for them to be stretched to lengths of twenty feet or longer, then hung on rods to dry. In the form of comedic storytelling *Rakugo*, there are stories of people draping the long noodles over their ears and neck or hanging them from upstairs windows and running downstairs to eat them from the bottom up, though this seems like a choking hazard and I would not recommend it. *Somen* were also the favorite noodle of fourteenth-century athletes. Banquets featuring large bowls of *somen* were eaten before matches of *sumai no sechie* at the imperial court. While you may think it odd to eat a bunch of noodles before an athletic performance, keep in mind this was an early form of sumo, so carbo loading was probably a major benefit for the contestants.

Today *somen* are the star of Tanabata, or the Star Festival, held in July. Introduced to Japan by the Empress Kōken in 755, the festival celebrates the reunion of the lovers Orihime and Hikoboshi (represented by the stars Vega and Altair), who are allowed to meet only once a year. Orihime, daughter of the king of the sky, was a weaver of beautiful cloth. Her father loved the cloth, and Orihime, wishing to please him, spent all day, every day, weaving, but in a time before dating apps this left her no time to meet a man and fall in love. Her father felt bad about this and set her up with Hikoboshi, a cowherd who lived on the other side of the river (as they lived in the sky, this river

continues

Nyumen

continued

Tanabata festival in Edo in 1852 by Hiroshige

was the Milky Way). The two instantly fell in love and married, but in their wedded bliss Orihime gave up weaving and Hikoboshi let his cows wander all over the sky. Tentei, clearly having no concept of the honeymoon period, was less than thrilled and decided to separate the two, placing one on either side of the Milky Way. Orihime was distraught and, rather than weaving, wept day and night, so her father decided that, provided she finished her weaving by the seventh day of the seventh month, the two lovers could reunite for that one day each year. What a mensch. So on July 7 every year, when the two stars meet in the sky, people eat *somen*. One noodle represents the thread Orihime weaves her cloth from, and when collected in a bowl the swirling noodles are reminiscent of the Milky Way that parts the lovers the other 364 days of the year. During the festival, the noodles are dipped in ice water and eaten cold. This recipe, from the seventeenth-century *Ryori Monogatari*, calls for them to be eaten hot, which makes it more of a daily meal.

MAKES 2 OR 3 SERVINGS   **COOK TIME:** 1 HOUR

FOR THE *TAREMISO*:
4 tablespoons (60 g) red or white miso paste

1 cup (250 ml) water

1. Make the *taremiso*: Combine the miso paste and water in a small saucepan and stir to dissolve. Set it over a low heat and simmer gently until the liquid is reduced to ⅔ of a cup, about 15 minutes. Do not let it boil. Once the *taremiso* is reduced, strain it through a piece of cheesecloth and cool it to room temperature.

continues

Nyumen

continued

FOR THE DASHI:
2 quarts (2 liters) water

1.75 ounces (50 g) kombu (dried kelp)

1.5 ounces (40 g) *katsuobushi* (bonito flakes)

4 tablespoons (60 ml) sake, optional

1 cup mustard greens

1 cup sliced Japanese eggplant

150 g *somen* noodles

Soy sauce or salt, as desired

½ cup sliced green onion

Freshly ground black pepper

Sansho pepper (or substitute Szechuan peppercorn) ground into powder

2. Make the dashi: Fill a pot with the water and soak the kombu until softened, about 30 minutes. If there is a white powder on the kombu, do not remove it, as that is where most of the flavor is. Once the kombu is soft, set the pot over medium heat and slowly bring to a simmer. Just before the water comes to a full boil, remove the kombu from the pot with tongs and discard. With the water boiling, add the *katsuobushi* and allow to boil for 30 seconds, then remove the pot from the heat and allow the *katsuobushi* to steep until most of the flakes have fallen to the bottom of the pot, about 10 minutes. Strain the dashi into another pot using either a strainer or cheesecloth for a clearer broth. Discard the *katsuobushi* flakes. If you are using sake, stir it into the strained dashi. Set the pot over medium heat and bring to a simmer for 1 minute, then remove from the heat and set aside.

3. While the *taremiso* and dashi cool, prepare the mustard greens and eggplant. Wash them well, then boil, steam, or grill them to your desired texture.

4. Boil water in a separate pot and add the *somen* noodles, allowing them to cook for 2 to 3 minutes or until soft. Strain the water out and immediately rinse the noodles in cold water. Set aside.

5. With all of the ingredients prepared, mix the *taremiso* into the dashi, and return the pot to the stove over medium heat. Once the dashi-*taremiso* mixture is warm, taste it and add soy sauce or salt, as desired. Once the mixture begins to simmer, add the noodles to the dashi to warm them for 30 seconds. Do not allow the dashi to boil. Remove the pot from the heat and dish the noodles into bowls, ladling the dashi-*taremiso* mixture over them. Add the cooked vegetables and green onion. Sprinkle with black pepper and Sansho pepper to taste and serve.

Cook's Note: The *taremiso* and dashi can be made up to one week ahead of time and kept refrigerated.

Little Meat Cakes

XXXXXXXXXXXXXXX

City/Region: Chinese
Mongol Empire
Time Period: c. 1330

> **FROM HISTORY**
>
> *Select mutton, 10 chin; remove the fat,
> membrane, and sinew. Mash into a paste with
> asafetida three ch'ien, black pepper two liang,
> long pepper one liang, finely ground coriander
> one liang. For ingredients use salt. Adjust
> flavors evenly. Use the fingers to make cakes.
> Put into vegetable oil and fry.*
>
> —Hu Sihui, *Yinshan Zhengyao* (translated by Paul. D. Buell)[1]

Genghis Khan

This recipe comes from Hu Sihui's dietary treatise, *Yinshan Zheng-yao*, written for the Chinese Mongol Empire in the early fourteenth century. Like many of the recipes in the work, this one has influences from all over the empire built by the great Genghis Khan. The lamb is very Mongolian, the pepper, Chinese, the "asafetida" would have likely come from what is now Afghanistan, and the dish itself is similar to the *köfte* still served in Turkey today. While *Yinshan Zhengyao* was written for the great Khan's descendants, it's likely Genghis himself enjoyed similar dishes near the end of his life, when cooks and ingredients from all over the empire came flowing into his kitchens. A far cry from the cuisine of his youth.

The food options on the Central Asian steppe in twelfth-century northern Mongolia were limited. For meat, the nomadic tribes lived off of what they could hunt: Bactrian camels, wolves, snow leopards, reindeer, bears, marmots, and game birds. They would only eat the meat of their herd animals, like horses, sheep, and goats, when absolutely necessary, preferring instead to use the milk of the animals to make butter and *qurut*, dried curds pressed between rocks to form a firm cheese. The drink of choice also came from milk, specifically mare's milk, which was fermented and turned into the lightly alcoholic *airag* or kumiss. Though even these were delicacies compared to what Temüjin, the boy who would grow up to be Genghis Khan, would have lived off after being left, with his mother and siblings, to die on the Mongolian plains following his father's death. And most would have died, but most did not have a mother like Üjin:

continues

Little Meat Cakes

continued

She went collecting the wild apples and the bird cherries
day and night she nourished their throats . . .
Digging up garden burnet and cinquefoil roots
Mother Üjin's children, nourished with wild garlic and
wild onions,
Managed to grow up to become khans . . .
To nourish their mother . . .
They went fishing with hooks for miserable fish.
Bending a fish hook from a needle.
—"Secret History of the Khans" (translated by Paul. D. Buell)[2]

And perhaps it was that rough childhood that forged him into the conqueror he would become, who led the Mongols out of the steppes to conquer much of Asia, both the land and the cuisine. It was only a couple generations after Genghis passed that his descendants were enjoying the fruits (and spices) of their ancestor's labor in dishes such as these wonderful "little meat cakes."

MAKES 12 MEAT CAKES   **COOK TIME:** 25 MINUTES

Soybean oil or other vegetable oil for frying (see Cook's Note)

1 pound (450 g) ground lamb

¼ teaspoon ground asafetida (see page 12)

2 teaspoons freshly ground black pepper

1 teaspoon ground long pepper (see page 13)

1 teaspoon ground coriander seed

1 teaspoon kosher salt

1. Heat 1½ inches (4 cm) of oil in a medium skillet over medium heat to a temperature of 350°F/175°C.

2. In a medium bowl, mix the ground lamb with asafetida, black pepper, long pepper, coriander, and salt and form the mixture into a dozen cakes of equal size. They should be about ¾ inch (2 cm) thick and will puff up once fried.

3. Add several cakes to the oil, not crowding the pan, and leave them undisturbed for 2 minutes. The cakes may puff up soon after going into the oil so that they are no longer submerged, but that is okay. After 2 minutes, use tongs to flip the cakes over to fry on the other side until they are a deep golden brown, about 1½ minutes.

4. Remove the cakes from the oil and set on a plate lined with paper towel to drain. Repeat until all of the cakes are fried.

Cook's Note: The original recipe does not specify a type of oil other than "vegetable oil." This does not mean the processed vegetable oil of today but merely refers to any oil that is not an animal product. In this case, it was likely soybean oil.

Gajeyuk

City/Region: Korea
Time Period: c. 1670

FROM HISTORY

Slice pork in thick and short pieces then marinate with soy sauce and oil. Coat it with flour and fry it. Serve it with black pepper.

—Jang Gye-hyang, *Eumsikdimibang*

This simple but delicious recipe for fried pork comes from one of Korea's oldest cookbooks, *Eumsikdimibang* (음식디미방). It's also one of Asia's first cookbooks written by a woman, Jang Gye-hyang.

Born in 1598, during the Joseon Dynasty, Jang Gye-hyang was part of the *yangban* caste, the wealthy caste of society just below the ruling class. Her father, Jang Huenghyo, was a famous teacher of the neo-Confuciansim philosophy, and while girls were excluded from higher learning, Jang would eavesdrop on her father's classes and sneak into his library to read his books. Through her covert learning, she taught herself to paint and write poetry. At the age of nine, she wrote a poem called "Ode to the Saint," the saint being the great scholars of the past. In it, she laments being unable to meet them but rejoices in the fact that she can glimpse into their psyche via the writings they left behind. What were you doing at nine years old?

While her career as a poet never came to fruition, her brilliance has forever been enshrined in *Eumsikdimibang*, which she wrote around 1670, when she was in her early seventies.

She wrote it with her failing eyesight as a guide for the wives of her seven sons, so they could keep her children well-fed. It includes two very different types of recipes showing two very different types of Korea at the time. Most belong to the *Joseon Wangjo Gungjung yori*, or the cuisine of the Korean royal court. These were dishes only available to those at the top of the social ladder, where Jang spent her life. At the other end of the spectrum are the sixteen recipes she calls *Matjilbangmun*. They were recipes for food of the common people and came from the village of Matjil, her mother's hometown. *Eumsikdimibang*, while focusing on the food of the wealthy, recognizes and respects those dishes that many in Jang's caste would have seen as beneath them, and that was evident in Jang's life as well as her cooking.

continues

Gajeyuk

continued

In 1636, when Korea was invaded by the Manchu-led Qing Dynasty, the war left many at the bottom of society displaced and starving. While her family was relatively untouched, Jang took in many of those displaced people and she planted groves of acorn trees around the village to feed those who were starving. In the evening, she would look down at the village, and the people of any household that did not have smoke rising from their kitchen would be invited up to the house for dinner, as she held the belief that it was a moral duty for those with wealth to share it with those less fortunate. And in *Eumsikdimibang* she has shared her wealth of knowledge with those who came after her, including us in the twenty-first century.

MAKES 4 SERVINGS **COOK TIME:** 40 MINUTES

1 pound (450 g) pork tenderloin

¼ cup (60 ml) soy sauce

2 tablespoons (30 ml) sesame oil

1 cup (140 g) whole wheat flour

Soybean oil, divided

Pinch freshly ground black pepper

OPTIONAL GARNISH:
1 inch fresh ginger

3 cloves garlic

¼ cup chopped scallion greens

1. Slice the pork tenderloin into ¼-inch-thick slices, then put it in a plastic bag. Pour in the soy sauce and sesame oil and shake the bag to coat the pork in the marinade, then let marinate for 30 minutes.

2. Prepare a small bowl of whole wheat flour. Coat the bottom of a frying pan in cooking oil and heat over medium-high heat. When the pork has marinated, lightly coat each slice with the flour, then set them in the frying pan. Fry each side until golden brown and cooked through, 1 to 2 minutes. Serve immediately sprinkled with fresh pepper.

3. For the optional garnish: Wash and slice the ginger and garlic as thin as possible. Coat the bottom of a small frying pan with cooking oil and heat over medium heat. Add the sliced ginger and garlic and fry for 1 minute, then remove them from the pan and mix with the chopped scallion greens. Set this garnish on top of the Gajeyuk.

Makshufa

City/Region: Baghdad
Time Period: c. 13th century

FROM HISTORY

The way to make it is to take equal parts sugar, almonds or pistachios, honey and sesame oil. Pound the sugar and almonds and mix them together. Take enough saffron to color it and add it with rose-water. Then throw the sesame oil in the dist so that it boils and boils up. Put the honey on it and stir it until foam appears, and throw the sugar and almonds on the honey. Stir continuously on a quiet fire until it is nearly thickened, and take it up.

—Muhammad b.al-Husan,
Kitab al-Tabikh (translated by Charles Perry)[1]

Makshufa is a sweet nut-filled candy from medieval Baghdad, and just like any candy, the most important ingredient is sugar. As early as 8000 BCE sugarcane was eaten on the island of New Guinea, and it slowly spread through the islands of Indonesia before arriving in India, where it was called *sarkara*. It became part of the ancient system of medicine Ayurveda. Originally, it was eaten by cutting a stalk of cane and sucking the sweet nectar from it, but by the first century CE, India had developed a way to crystallize the sugar and refine it into something similar to what we know today. The Guptas called this crystallized sugar *khanda*, which is where we get the modern word "candy."

During Alexander the Great's invasion of India, around 325 BCE, his general Nearchus wrote of a reed that gave honey without the need of bees, and when they returned to Europe, they brought news of sugar with them. Greek physicians included it in their medical texts as a treatment for kidney stones or upset stomach, and Pliny the Elder touts Indian sugar as being especially good, but still only for medical purposes. It wasn't until the seventh century that Arabian cooks decided it could be used as a replacement, albeit an expensive one, for honey, and as the first caliphs conquered their way across North Africa and into Spain they left a trail of sugar refineries

continues

Makshufa

continued

behind them. In the thirteenth century, a German monk named Burchard of Mount Zion gave an account of how these refineries worked:

> *The canes are gathered, cut in lengths of half a palm,*
> *and so are crushed in the press. The juice squeezed out*
> *of them is boiled in copper boilers, and when thickened,*
> *is collected in baskets made of slender twigs. Soon after*
> *this it becomes dry and hard, and this is how sugar is made.*
> *Before it dries, a liquor oozes from it, called honey of sugar,*
> *which is very delicious and good for flavoring cakes.*
> —*Descriptio Terrae Sanctae*

And while it remained an elusive ingredient in European cooking, reserved only for the most wealthy, the sugar Brother Burchard describes was a staple ingredient of the Islamic world. The medieval Egyptian historian Al-Maqrizi claimed the Mamluk sultans of twelfth-century Egypt ate three hundred tons of it each month. Luckily, for this recipe for Makshufa, you'll only need a little more than a cup.

MAKES 25 TO 35 CANDIES   **COOK TIME:** 45 MINUTES

2 cups (250 g) unsalted, shelled pistachios or blanched almonds

1⅓ cup (265 g) granulated sugar

Pinch of saffron threads

3 tablespoons (45 ml) rosewater

1 cup (240 ml) sesame oil (untoasted)

⅔ cup (160 ml) honey

Sesame seeds, optional

1. Line a large baking sheet with aluminum foil lightly sprayed with nonstick spray and set aside.

2. Using a food processor, grind the nuts into a powder, then add the sugar and mix until incorporated. Add the saffron and rosewater and mix. Pour the sesame oil into a large saucepan and set over medium-high heat. Heat for 5 minutes, then reduce heat to low and pour in the honey, stirring to combine. Allow to simmer until a light layer of foam forms all over the top, about 5 minutes.

3. Carefully, add the nut and sugar mixture, making sure to not to let the oil splash. Stir the mixture together until it becomes homogenous. Raise the heat to medium and continue to stir while the mixture heats and begins to thicken, about 15 minutes. Using a candy thermometer or instant-read thermometer, stir until the mixture reaches 270°F/132°C. For a slightly darker and less sweet candy, heat for another 10 degrees, but do not let it pass 290°F/143°C or the mixture will burn.

continues

Makshufa

continued

4. Once the candy reaches the desired temperature, remove the saucepan from the heat and spread the entire mixture over the baking sheet, which can then be broken into shards like peanut brittle. Alternately, working quickly, spoon large dollops onto the prepared baking sheet. If you are using sesame seeds to garnish, sprinkle them over the candy before it cools.

5. Allow the mixture to cool completely, about 20 minutes, then serve. If not serving immediately, keep the Makshufa in the refrigerator, as it will become very sticky and lose its sheen if left at room temperature.

Burchard of Mount Zion in the Holy Land from *Descriptio Terrae Sanctae* (1283)

Hummus
Kassa

City/Region: Egypt
Time Period: c. 14th century

FROM HISTORY

Hummus Kassa—Take boiled chickpeas and pound them into fine mush. Add vinegar, sweet olive oil, tahini, black pepper, atraf tib, mint, Macedonian parsley, and a bit of dried rue. Also add walnuts, almonds, pistachios, and hazelnuts—all pounded—as well as Ceylon cinnamon, toasted caraway seeds, coriander, salt, lemon preserved in salt, and olives. Mix it all, spread the mix in a bowl or plate, set it aside for a day and then serve. It will come out good, God willing.

—*Kanz al-fawa'id fi tanwi al-mawa'id* or
Treasure Trove of Benefits and Variety at the Table
(translated by Nawal Nasrallah)[1]

I never could have conceived of a recipe for hummus as complicated as this one from fourteenth-century Egypt. Today most hummus recipes have four or five ingredients, but this one has nearly thirty if you include the complex spice mixture known as Atraf Tib or Atraf al-Tib. The dish's preparation is an undertaking, at least as far as hummus is concerned, but in my opinion, that's what sets it apart and makes it worthy of inclusion in this book.

The source for the recipe, *Kanz al-fawa'id fi tanwi al-mawa'id*, offers a fascinating look into Egypt seven hundred years ago. The book starts out with directions on keeping a kitchen clean and laying out the traits of a good cook:

The cook should be an agreeable person. . . . He needs to keep his fingernails trimmed at all times. However, he should clip them neither too short and cause injuries, nor let them grow long enough to trap dirt underneath them.[2]

continues

Hummus Kassa

continued

Seven centuries on and this is still an excellent way to weed out candidates for a job in the kitchen. After a bit more good-sense advice on how to run a kitchen and handle food, the extensive list of recipes begins, sometimes accompanied by advice that may be less than useful, but quite interesting, to today's reader. These include avoiding drinking water first thing after waking up or during a meal or after a meal, especially cold water, as it is likely to cool down the liver too much. That said, cold water is okay, even when eating, for "those who have a lot of flesh, whose blood is red and whose appetites are strong."[3] I suppose that puts me in the clear.

Though if you're not supposed to drink water, then what do you drink? *Fuqqa.* The book contains over a dozen recipes for the foamy beer known as *fuqqa*, a popular alcoholic beverage in medieval Egypt. These could be flavored with, among other things, mint, pomegranate, pepper, or cardamom, though he warns that, delicious as these beers are, they are likely to cause headaches and flatulence. One thing that will stand out to any modern reader of the *Kanz al-fawa'id* is the number of recipes that are accompanied by a warning of impending flatulence. Even the plain cold water doesn't escape without the caveat. So of course, it's no shock that I must offer the same word of caution with this hummus recipe, as the author singles out chickpeas as a particular culprit, but I assure you, it's worth it.

continues

Hummus Kassa

continued

FOR THE ATRAF TIB:

2 small, dried bay leaves

1 teaspoon dried rosebuds

1 teaspoon dried spikenard root (see page 13)

1 teaspoon ground ginger

1 teaspoon ground cardamom

½ teaspoon ground nutmeg

½ teaspoon ground mace

½ teaspoon ground betel nut

½ teaspoon ground long pepper (see page 13)

½ teaspoon freshly ground black pepper

⅛ teaspoon ground clove

FOR THE HUMMUS:

1 cup (200 g) dried chickpeas

4 tablespoons (60 g) tahini

2 tablespoons (30 ml) white wine vinegar

3 tablespoons (45 ml) extra-virgin olive oil, plus more for garnish

¼ teaspoon freshly ground black pepper

½ cup chopped pitted olives

¼ cup (30 g) raw, unsalted walnut halves, plus more for garnish

¼ cup (30 g) shelled raw, unsalted almonds, plus more for garnish

¼ cup (45 g) shelled raw, unsalted pistachios, plus more for garnish

¼ cup (30 g) whole raw, unsalted hazelnuts, plus more for garnish

1. Make the Atraf Tib: Grind the bay leaves, rosebuds, and spikenard, then, in a small bowl, whisk them with the ginger, cardamom, nutmeg, mace, betel, long pepper, black pepper, and clove. This will yield far more than you need for this recipe, but making any less proves difficult to measure. Bottle it and it will keep.

2. Make the hummus: Soak the chickpeas in cool water for eight hours. Then drain and rinse them and place them in a medium saucepan. Add clean water until the chickpeas are covered with 4 inches of water. Set the saucepan over medium heat and bring to a simmer. Cover and simmer until the chickpeas can easily be mashed with a spoon, about 90 minutes. Remove from the heat and drain any excess water. Allow the chickpeas to cool.

3. Once the chickpeas are cooled, mash them or blend in a food processor. For a smoother hummus, remove the skins of each chickpea before blending, but this is not necessary. Stir the tahini into ½ cup (120 ml) of cold water until mostly dissolved and then mix it into the chickpeas along with the white wine, olive oil, and black pepper. If you are using a food processor or blender, which I recommend, add the olives, walnuts, almonds, pistachios, hazelnuts, mint, parsley, lemon, Atraf Tib, rue, salt, cinnamon, caraway, and coriander and blend until smooth. If you are mixing the hummus together by hand, first grind the nuts, olives, and preserved lemon as finely as possible before adding them to the Atraf Tib and hummus. Once all are combined and smooth, spoon the hummus onto a plate and spread it out evenly, then cover with foil and refrigerate at least eight hours to let the flavors combine.

3 tablespoons finely chopped fresh mint leaves, plus more for garnish

3 tablespoons finely chopped fresh parsley leaves, plus more for garnish

¼ salt-preserved lemon, finely chopped

1 teaspoon Atraf Tib

1 teaspoon dried rue (see page 13)

¾ teaspoon kosher salt

¼ teaspoon ground cinnamon

¼ teaspoon ground caraway seeds

¼ teaspoon ground coriander

4. When you're ready to serve, allow the hummus to come to room temperature, then garnish with additional nuts and herbs and drizzle with olive oil.

Cook's Note: Atraf Tib was a popular spice mix in medieval Islamic cuisine and appears in most cookbooks of the time, though rarely are the ingredients in the mixture defined. This assortment is based on one thirteenth-century description, but as it likely changed from place to place and throughout time, do not feel compelled to use all of the spices or in any specific quantities. It can be personalized to the cook.

The
NEW
WORLD

✕✕✕✕✕

Tamales

City/Region: Mexico
Time Period: c. 1520

Aztecs eating tamales from
the *Florentine Codex*

Tamales were a staple of the diet of many Mesoamerican cultures and are depicted as far back as the first century in Mayan murals, but this first written description of water tamales, by the Spanish Franciscan friar Bernardino de Sahagún, sounds horribly bland. No salt, no chili, and not nixtamalized (a process discussed later in the recipe for Quesadillas Cernidas, page 219). But the feast where they were eaten, Atamalqualiztli, was anything but bland. As a prologue to the tamales, Sahagún says people ate live snakes and frogs, then made offerings and dined on water tamales.

But our tamales won't include a prelude of snakes or a coda of live frogs. In fact, I'm determined to stay away from the water tamales altogether. Rather, I look to other fillings Sahagún mentions in his *General History of the Things of New Spain*, which include fruit, chili sauce, and the meat of turkeys and the hairless Xoloitzcuintle dog. Worry not. I won't be sending you on the search for dog meat for this recipe. They also likely used corn oil to bind their dough rather than the lard often used today, as the fatty pig that provides lard was an import from the Spanish. The Spanish also brought the beef and domesticated chickens that fill most tamales today. But it took some time for the Spanish colonists to come around to

continues

Tamales

continued

eating tamales, as most of the foods enjoyed by the native population were seen to be inferior to those of the Europeans. Even as late as 1915, in Carlos González Peña's novel *La fuga de la quimera*, eating tamales was used as a symbol of the main character's moral decay into a licentious affair.

In the United States, though, the stigma did not follow and, especially in those states that had once been part of Mexico, tamales were prized and reserved for holidays and special occasions. They were a featured food at the Chicago World's Columbian Exposition in 1893, which spurred their popularity throughout the country. By the 1920s, from California to Florida, tamale men could be heard shouting, "Red hots for sale!" But the proliferation of these street vendors led to the occasional butting of heads over sales territory, which escalated into what newspapers of the day termed "The Tamale Wars." And the term "wars" wasn't entirely sensationalist, as evidenced by one incident in Omaha, Nebraska, in 1921:

Weston and Lewis were members of two competitive "hot tamale rings" . . . On the fateful night the rival peddlers of the two factions had declared a truce for the party but during the evening the truce was broken by someone who sank an axe several times into the head of Lewis.
—*Omaha Daily Bee*, December 16, 1921

But today the violent tamale craze has fizzled and now they're most often made by peaceful *abuelas* hosting *tamaladas*, or tamale-making parties, in the weeks leading up to Christmas.

MAKES 30 TO 40 TAMALES   **COOK TIME:** 3 HOURS

30 to 40 packaged dried corn husks

FOR THE FILLING:
Fruit such as papaya or pumpkin

Sea salt, to taste

Turkey, boiled or roasted

Diced chiles, to taste

Chili sauce, optional

1. Fill a wide bowl with hot water and soak the corn husks, placing something heavy on them to keep them submerged, for 30 minutes or until softened. Remove them from the water and pat them dry with a paper towel, then set aside.

2. Prepare the filling: Sahagún mentions both fruit and turkey being used, undoubtedly separately, so feel free to make one or the other or both. For the fruit, steam or roast it until softened and then mash and mix with a little salt, to taste. For the turkey, roast or boil it until the meat can be easily shredded. Then mix with diced chiles, to taste, and season with salt. More modern fillings would call for seasoned beef, chicken, or pork, so feel free to use any filling you like.

FOR THE DOUGH:
3 cups (700 ml) water (see Cook's Note)

2 teaspoons ground tequesquite (or 1½ teaspoons baking powder)

4 cups (600 g) masa harina

1½ teaspoons sea salt

1⅓ cups corn oil

Cook's Note: For added flavor, use the modern option of chicken broth in lieu of water.

3. Make the dough: Heat the water in a medium saucepan over medium-low heat to a simmer and stir in the ground tequesquite until dissolved (if you're substituting baking powder, you will add it directly to the masa harina). In a large bowl, mix the masa harina and salt, then add the warm water and corn oil and mix until you form a soft, spreadable dough, similar to the consistency of peanut butter. For a smoother, fluffier dough, mix the dough using a stand mixer. If the dough is not that consistency, add more water, 1 tablespoon at a time, until it is. Cover the bowl with a damp towel to stop the dough from drying out as you assemble the tamales.

4. To form the tamales, place a corn husk with the smoother, glossy side up and spoon 3 or 4 tablespoons of the corn dough into the center of the husk. Use a spoon to spread the dough to about ¼ inch thick, making sure to keep the dough away from the sides of the husk and only on the top half (the wider half) of the husk. Spoon 1 or 2 tablespoons of the filling in a line down of the center of the dough.

5. Fold one long side of the husk over the filling and then the other long side over that, similar to how you might fold a letter. Then fold the bottom of the husk up and set the tamale aside. Repeat until all of the dough and filling has been used.

6. Add a couple cups of hot water to the bottom of your steamer, along with a coin. The coin will begin to rattle once the water is boiling and if it stops rattling you will know to add more water. Set the rack in the steamer and line the bottom with corn husks. Fill the steamer with the tamales standing upright, the open end facing up. Cover the tamales with additional corn husks and the lid of the steamer. Set over high heat and bring to a boil. Once the water is boiling, reduce the heat to allow it to simmer for 50 to 60 minutes, depending on the size of your steamer. At 50 minutes, remove one tamale from the steamer and try to remove the husk. If it easily comes away, that means they are done. If it sticks or the filling looks too wet, then return it to the pot and continue to cook for 10 minutes, then try again. The tamales can be served alone or with a chili sauce.

History Fact: In 1911, during the Mexican Revolution, the revolutionary Pascual Orozco stripped the uniforms of the dead soldiers he'd caught after ambush and sent the clothes to Presidente Díaz with a note saying: "Here are the wrappers, send me more tamales."

Aztec Chocolate

City/Region: Mexico
Time Period: c. 1520

> ### FROM HISTORY
>
> *The seller of fine chocolate . . . she grinds cacao; she crushes them. She separates them. She soaks them. She adds water sparingly . . . pours it back and forth, aerates it; she makes it form a head of foam.*
>
> —Bernardino de Sahagún,
> *General History of the Things of New Spain*[1]

Deer receives cacao from his wife, Snake, from Codex Zouche-Nuttall

The Aztecs loved their *xocolatl.* The Spanish friar Bernardino de Sahagún gives us this general idea of how they made their famous chocolate drink and says it was often flavored with flowers, honey, achiote, chile peppers, vanilla, allspice, and other ingredients you'd likely not find in hot chocolate today.

But to the Aztecs, cacao beans were so much more than just the base for a delicious drink. They were a precious commodity that, at times, acted as currency. In 1545, a market in Mexico City sold a turkey for one hundred cacao beans, a rabbit for thirty, a chicken egg for two, and one cacao bean could buy you a single tamale. And as with any currency, counterfeit cacao beans were a problem. Sahagún describes how unscrupulous cacao sellers would carve wax or avocado pits into the shape of cacao beans, wrap them in discarded cacao bean hulls, then sell them on to unsuspecting customers.

But this counterfeiter better hope one of his faux cacao beans doesn't end up in the kitchens of the great Moctezuma II, who drank *xocolatl* to excess:

> *After the hot dishes had been removed, every kind of fruit which the country produced was set on the table; of which, however, Montezuma ate very little. Every now and then a golden vessel was handed to him filled with a kind of liquor made from the cacao, which is meant for success with women. . . . I saw about fifty large pitchers filled with the same liquor brought in all frothy. This beverage was also presented to the monarch by*

continues

Aztec Chocolate

continued

women, but all with the profoundest veneration. . . . After the Great Montezuma had dined, dinner was served to the men of the Guard and the other household officers, and I have often counted, on the table, over a thousand dishes. . . . These were followed by over two thousand frothing jugs of cacao drink.
—Bernal Diaz del Castillo, *The Memoirs of the Conquistador Bernal Diaz del Castillo Written by Himself Containing a True and Full Account of the Discovery and Conquest of Mexico and New Spain*

Though, while Diaz claims the vessels were gold, other authors say that they were cups made of calabash gourds that were treated as if they were gold, so as you re-create the Aztec emperor's favorite beverage, feel free to use any cup you have available.

MAKES 4 SERVINGS   **COOK TIME:** 20 MINUTES

¾ cup (80 g) cacao nibs

2 red chile peppers

1 quart (1 liter) water

1 vanilla pod or 2 teaspoons (30 ml) vanilla extract

⅓ cup (80 ml) honey or agave syrup

½ teaspoon allspice

Cook's Note: Before you begin, feel free to alter these ingredients to suit your taste. Add more honey or agave syrup for a sweeter *xocolatl*, or remove the peppers altogether for a less spicy drink. This can also be served warm or at room temperature.

1. Using a spice grinder, grind the cacao nibs into a fine powder. It may begin to liquify, which is fine, if not preferred. Set aside.

2. Roughly chop the chiles, discarding the stems, and add both flesh and seeds to a medium saucepan with the water over high heat. Bring the water to a low boil, reducing the heat as necessary, for 5 minutes. Pour the chile water through a strainer into another saucepan and discard the chiles. Set the saucepan over low heat and scrape in the vanilla seeds (or add the vanilla extract); add the honey and allspice. Mix until dissolved. Bring the water to a simmer and add the ground cacao nibs. Whisk until dissolved, then allow to simmer for 5 minutes. Pour the drink into mugs and use a whisk or *molinillo* to froth. For more of a froth, replace half of the water with milk, which would have been available shortly after the conquest.

Doctors lay by your Irksome Books
And all ye Petty-Fogging Rookes
Leave Quacking; and Enucleate
The virtues of our Chocolate.
—Antonio Colmenero de Ledesma, *Chocolate: or, An Indian Drinke* (1652)

Quesadillas Cernidas

City/Region: Mexico
Time Period: 1831

FROM HISTORY

Put your corn to cook with water, rinse and let it dry. Grind it and sift. Mix with the dough a little melted lard, salt, and little of the settled tequesquite so the dough is workable. Sprinkle with flour and form into a disk, well flattened, and put a little aged cheese, or fresh, according to your preference. Fold over the edges so they stick. At this point put them into very hot lard, bathing continuously each so they puff up. Take them out and drain them and eat them fresh.

—Anonymous, *El cocinero mexicano*

Aztecs growing maize from the *Florentine Codex*

Quesadillas get their name from their cheesy insides, but in this recipe it's the crisp fried corn tortilla that steals the show. And while the cheese was introduced to Mexican cuisine by the Spanish, the corn, or maize, has been a staple of the Mesoamerican diet since time immemorial. According to the Mayan creation myth described in the *Popul Vuh*, maize was there at the very beginning when the gods used it to literally make humans. But the Aztecs were not so fortunate and had to rely on the feathered serpent god, Quetzalcoatl, to get it for them.

Legend has it that long ago, during the Fifth Sun, the Aztec people ate only what they could hunt and gather, but they knew of a plant called maize that grew on the other side of the insurmountable mountains surrounding their valley. They'd asked several of their gods to move the mountains so they could reach the maize, but either the mountains proved too large or the gods were just not that invested. But Quetzalcoatl, the feathered serpent god, remarked what so many infomercials of the early nineties did: "There's gotta be a better way!" So, seeing a red ant scurrying toward the mountains, he turned himself into a tiny black ant and followed it. After many days of perilous journeying, the two ants came out on the other side where the maize grew. Quetzalcoatl picked up a kernel of maize in his little

continues

Quesadillas Cernidas

continued

ant pincers and headed back through the mountains and to the Aztec people, who took it and were no doubt grateful for the gift, but I imagine they were slightly irked that the god hadn't turned himself into a slightly larger animal that could carry more than one kernel. As it was, they planted the kernel from which their staple crop grew. So before taking a bite out of your crunchy Quesadillas Cernidas, make sure to thank the feathered serpent god for thinking on his feet.

MAKES 10 TO 12 QUESADILLAS   **COOK TIME:** 45 MINUTES

1 tablespoon tequesquite (see Cook's Note)

1 cup (250 ml) warm and ¼ cup (60 ml) boiling water, divided

1½ cups (180 g) masa harina

1 teaspoon sea salt

2 tablespoons melted lard (or corn oil), plus more for frying

4 ounces (115 g) Oaxaca cheese or other mild cheese that will melt

Cook's Note: As a substitute for tequesquite, use 1 teaspoon baking soda dissolved in 2 tablespoons warm water.

1. Crush the tequesquite into a powder and pour ¼ cup boiling water over it and stir until dissolved as much as possible. Allow to sit for 10 minutes to allow any large particles to settle at the bottom of the bowl.

2. In a large bowl, whisk together the masa harina and salt, then add 1 cup warm water and the melted lard and mix to form a dough, which is called masa. Skim 2 tablespoons of the tequesquite water, trying not to get any of the large sediment at the bottom, and mix it into the dough. The dough should have the consistency of Play-Doh. If it sticks to your fingers, add more masa harina, 1 tablespoon at a time. If it is too dry and crumbly, add more water 1 tablespoon at a time. Cover the bowl with a damp towel and let rest for 10 minutes.

3. Shape the masa into 2 tablespoon-sized balls. Place a ball between two squares of parchment or two plastic bags. Use a rolling pin or tortilla press to press the ball into a thin tortilla about 5 inches (12.5 cm) across. The parchment/plastic should easily peel away from the tortilla without sticking. Repeat the process until all of the masa has been made into tortillas.

4. Sprinkle cheese on half of the tortilla, leaving ¾ of an inch bare around the edges, then fold over and press down to seal in the cheese, forming a quesadilla.

5. Heat lard or oil in a pan about a half inch deep over medium-high heat. When the lard has reached 350°F/175°C carefully place a quesadilla into the pan. Let it cook 1 minute, continuously spooning lard over the top, then use a spatula to flip the quesadilla over to cook the other side while you spoon lard over the already-cooked side. Once the quesadilla has browned and puffed up a bit, remove from the oil and set on a paper towel to drain, then eat.

Gin Cocktail

✖✖✖✖✖✖✖✖✖✖✖✖✖✖

City/Region: United States
of America
Time Period: 1862

Jerry Thomas

My favorite liquor, a spirit flavored with juniper berry, began life in the Netherlands under the name *genever* (also spelled *jenever* or *genièvre*). At the end of the seventeenth century, the Netherlands made two key imports to England: Willem van Oranje and *genever*, both of which received a name change. Willem became William III of England and *genever* was shortened to "gin." As the new king enjoyed the drink, thought to be medicinal, gin gained in popularity over the more common ales drunk by the common man and the brandy that suffered from its association with France. Unfortunately, gin's popularity led to a deterioration of the product and its overconsumption. In 1714, Bernard de Mandeville wrote:

> *Nothing is more destructive, either in regard to the health*
> *or the vigilance and industry of the poor, than the infamous*
> *liquor . . . gin, that charms the inactive, the desperate and*
> *crazy of either sex, and makes the starving sot behold his*
> *rags and nakedness with stupid indolence, or banter both in*
> *senseless laughter, and more insipid jests!*
> —*The Fable of the Bees*

But even the finger wagging of the venerable de Mandeville couldn't stop what became known as "The London Gin Craze." And "craze" is an appropriate word, as the gin of the lower classes was often homemade and included

The Gin Shop by George Cruikshank

things like sulfuric acid and turpentine to give it an extra kick. At a time of rising poverty in London, it was this cheap gin that took the blame for a rise in violent crime, including a notorious murder in 1734.

One afternoon, Judith Defour and a friend, already drunk on gin and unable to afford more, took Judith's two-year-old daughter from the workhouse, where the little girl had been given new clothes. In Judith's own words from the trial:

We took the child into the fields, and stripp'd it, and ty'd a linen handkerchief hard about its neck to keep it from crying, and then laid it in a ditch. And after that, we went together, and sold the coat and stay for a shilling, and the petticoat and stockings for a groat. We parted the money, and join'd for a quatern of Gin.

Judith was found guilty and hanged at Tyburn and gin took much of the blame. The shocking incident led to new laws regulating and taxing the sale of gin, but the Craze continued unabated until 1751, when a piece of art tarnished gin's reputation even more than infanticide.

Beer Street and *Gin Lane* were two engravings printed by William Hogarth in support of the Gin Act. *Beer Street* is shown as inhabited by the industrious and artistic members of society, with everyone smiling as new buildings are constructed along the street. In contrast, *Gin Lane* is home to a mother with syphilitic sores mindlessly dropping her child down a stairwell as a man beside her fights a dog over a bone. The buildings are crumbling into the street as a pauper is lifted into a gin-induced early grave.

London's gin fever broke, and its consumption diminished until the mid-nineteenth century, when it became an ingredient in new cocktail recipes, like this one from the great Jerry Thomas.

MAKES 1 COCKTAIL   **COOK TIME:** 1 MINUTE

2 ounces (60 ml) London dry gin

1 teaspoon gum syrup

½ teaspoon orange curaçao

2 dashes Bogart's/Boker's bitters

1 inch fresh lemon peel

Fill a shaker half-full of ice. Add the gin, gum syrup, orange curaçao, bitters, and shake. Strain into a small rocks glass or cocktail glass. Twist the lemon peel over the cocktail and drop it in.

Cook's Note: Through the years, Jerry Thomas modified this recipe in quantities of ingredients and was inconsistent as to whether it should be shaken or stirred, so feel free to make it your own.

Bread Pudding

✕✕✕✕✕✕✕✕✕✕✕✕✕✕✕

City/Region: United States of America
Time Period: 1862

Joseph Janvier Woodward

I n the early days of the US Civil War, Dr. Joseph J. Woodward lamented the fact that his hospital stewards knew little about medicine and even less about cooking, and with no antibiotics or surgical antiseptic a decent meal was all most patients could rely on to bring them back to health:

Perhaps no subject is more worthy of attention in a hospital than the quality of the food and the character of the cooking. In the latter there is certainly greater room for improvement in the United States army hospitals than in the former.

And so a year into the war, Dr. Woodward wrote *The Hospital Steward's Manual*, a quick and easy guide to bring his stewards up to snuff. It begins with detailed instructions on how to keep the operating room and kitchen clean and borrows many techniques from Florence Nightingale, who, less than ten years earlier, during the Crimean War, had solved many of Woodward's problems in her own hospital. Then he lays out the meals of the convalescent, three meals a day of varying sizes. Starting at the "low diet," the ration consisted of just enough food to fend off starvations. The "half diet" was a bit more than that, and the "full diet" topped out at what most today would consider an appetizer. Most of the meals were a thin stew, bread and butter, or mush and milk with a cup of coffee, but on occasion, if a soldier was lucky or in dire need of it, he'd receive "extra diet." This could be eggs, chicken, fresh fruit, malt liquor, or bread pudding.

The manual finishes with recipes for all of the necessary dishes, many of which Woodward credits to the celebrated chef Alexis Soyer, who advised the English army how to cook during the Crimean War. The recipes are notable for their size; "Tea for eighty men" or "Bean Soup for one hundred men." But the bread pudding recipe that we're making only feeds about eight.

MAKES 8 SERVINGS   **COOK TIME:** 1 HOUR 30 MINUTES

2 cups (475 ml) whole milk

1 cinnamon stick

2 or 3 strips of lemon peel

¾ cup (60 g) small, loose bread crumbs from dry, stale wheat bread (it is best to measure these by weight)

2 large eggs, beaten, at room temperature

2 tablespoons (20 g) dried currants (see page 12)

2 tablespoons (25 g) dark brown sugar

1. Pour the milk into a small saucepan and add the cinnamon stick and lemon peel. Set over medium heat and bring to a boil for one minute.

2. Remove the cinnamon and lemon peel and pour the milk over the bread crumbs in a large bowl. Mix until the crumbs are well moistened. If the mixture is steaming, let it sit until just warm but not steaming, then slowly add the beaten eggs, mixing continuously until smooth and you have a batter. Add the currants and brown sugar and mix until well combined.

3. Boil a kettle of water while you prepare the pudding basin. Coat a small (1 liter) non-fluted pudding basin with nonstick cooking spray or a heavy coating of butter. Cut a small piece of parchment and line the bottom of the basin. Pour the batter into the basin and smooth the top.

4. Cut a large square of aluminum foil and a slightly smaller square of parchment paper. Set the paper on top of the aluminum foil. Make a pleat by folding a crease down the center of both sheets. This will allow the pudding to expand while cooking. The pleat should protrude on the aluminum foil side.

5. Place this, paper side down, over the pudding, then press the sides down around the bowl. With a long piece of string, tie the foil tightly around the lip of the basin. Trim any excess paper and press the foil in to form a watertight seal.

6. Make a handle by threading a double length of string through the string tied around the pudding. Pull it through the other side and tie it.

continues

Bread Pudding

continued

7. Put the basin in a pot and pour the boiling water around the pudding until it reaches halfway up the basin. Cover the pot and set it over medium heat. Steam for 1 hour. Keep an eye on the water level, making sure it never drops below ¼ of the way up the basin. When adding more water, make sure it is already-boiling water from the kettle. Never add cold water.

8. Once the pudding is steamed, remove the pot from the heat and carefully remove the pudding. Cut the string and remove the foil and paper. Allow the pudding to cool for 20 minutes, then run a knife around the edge to release it from the basin. Turn it out onto a plate and serve warm.

The Kitchen of the Fremont Dragoons

Egg Nog

XXXXXXXXXXXXXXXXXX

City/Region: United States
of America
Time Period: 1887

Humphrey Prideaux

Egg Nog. What an odd name. The egg part is obvious, but what in the world is nog? There are many theories. Some say the name came from the wooden cup, called a noggin, from which it may have been drunk, or *nugg*, which in Scotland referred to a cup of ale warmed with a red-hot poker. Perhaps Humphrey Prideaux had the right of it when he wrote, of the Dean of Norwich in 1693, that "you will find him walking about his room with a pipe in his mouth and a bottle of claret and a bottle of old strong beer (which in this country they call nog) upon the table" (*Letters of Humphrey Prideaux, Sometime Dean of Norwich, to John Ellis*). Whatever the truth is, the word didn't get married to "egg" until the eighteenth century.

The drink, which likely began in England as a descendant of posset, a concoction of egg with ale or wine that had been popular since the Middle Ages, was nonetheless always cited as an American invention in the cookbooks and cocktail books of the nineteenth century. Regardless of its origin, as far back as the 1790s, Egg Nog has always been associated with the American Christmas. On January 14, 1793, the *Virginia Chronicle* related a story:

> *On last Christmas Eve, several gentlemen met at Northampton*
> *court-house, and spent the evening in mirth and festivity,*
> *when EGG-NOG was the principal Liquor used by the*

continues

Egg Nog

continued

company. After they had indulged pretty freely in this beverage, a gentleman in company offered a bet that not one of the party could write four verses, extempore, which should be rhyme and sense . . .

Another partygoer accepted the challenge and recited, supposedly off the cuff, a poem extolling the virtues of Egg Nog over wine:

'Tis Egg-Nog now whose golden streams dispense
Far richer treasures to the ravish'd sense.
The Muse from Wine derives a transient glare,
But Egg-Nog's daughters afford her solid fare.

Personally, I can't imagine ever being able to compose such an homage, especially after an evening of drinking Egg Nog. Though, perhaps the nog in eighteenth-century Virginia was not as boozy as this recipe from 1887, for I promise, two cups of this wonderful beverage and you won't be able to recite poetry, let alone compose it.

MAKES 12 SERVINGS **COOK TIME:** 4 HOURS 30 MINUTES

10 large eggs

¾ cup (150 g) granulated sugar

1½ cups (350 ml) brandy

1½ cups (350 ml) rye whiskey

1 quart (1 liter) whole milk

2 cups (475 ml) heavy whipping cream

2 teaspoons ground nutmeg, plus more for garnish

1. Separate the eggs' whites and yolks into two large bowls. Beat the yolks until a pale yellow, then, while beating, add the sugar ¼ cup at a time, incorporating completely before adding the next ¼ cup. Slowly pour in the brandy while beating, then the rye whiskey. Stir in the milk, cream, and nutmeg until well combined.

2. Using clean beaters, beat the whites until you achieve soft peaks, then beat them into the Egg Nog ⅓ at a time. Cover the bowl with aluminum foil and set in the refrigerator for at least 4 hours, but preferably 3 to 5 days. The flavor will develop more the longer it is left.

3. This can be served cold or warmed up over the stove. Grate fresh nutmeg on top and serve in punch glasses.

Vinegar Candy

XXXXXXXXXXXXXXXXX

City/Region: United States of America
Time Period: 1896

Fannie Farmer

Vinegar candy may not sound appealing at first, but with a quality apple cider vinegar it is the perfect blend of sweet and sour. In addition, making it involves the age-old tradition of the taffy pull, an exhausting yet wonderful activity, fun for the whole family and a great way to keep the kids occupied around the holidays. This particular recipe is one of the many well-written recipes from the mother of the American recipe, Fannie Farmer.

Fannie Merritt Farmer was born in Boston in 1857, but at the age of sixteen she suffered a paralytic stroke, which took her out of school. With limited mobility, she was stuck at her parents' home with little to occupy her other than watching her mother cook and, I assume, pulling taffy. But the long hours in the kitchen led Fannie to develop her own skills as a cook and soon she convinced her parents to turn their home into a boardinghouse, one that became renowned for its excellent meals, courtesy of Fannie herself.

By thirty, she had regained her ability to walk on her own, albeit with a limp that she would have the rest of her life, and she decided to further her culinary education by attending the Boston Cooking School. At that time, the school catered to the domestic cooks who worked for the middle-class and wealthy families of Boston. The curriculum was on the cutting edge of the Domestic Science Movement, which focused on the science, sometimes pseudoscience, of food, looking at the chemical makeup of ingredients and their influence on diet and nutrition, and this is what intrigued Ms. Farmer.

Cooking class in nineteenth-century Boston

While at school, the students worked from a cookbook written by a former principal, Mary J. Lincoln. After several years at the school, Fannie ended up becoming principal herself, and she reworked Mrs. Lincoln's book to create *The Boston Cooking School Cook Book* in 1896. The publisher, Little, Brown & Company, did not believe in the commercial viability of the book and would only print three thousand copies, which Fannie had to pay for herself. In doing so, she retained all of the rights to the book, which would go on to sell hundreds of thousands of copies during her lifetime and make her a tidy profit.

What made Fannie Farmer's cookbook stand out over all others was that her recipes were written with a precision rarely seen in previous decades, allowing the dishes to be easily replicated by even the most amateur home cook. Even before the first recipe appears in the book, Ms. Farmer instructs the reader on how to measure properly:

> *Good judgment, with experience, has taught some to measure by sight; but the majority need definite guides. . . . To measure a cupful, put in the ingredient by spoonfuls or from a scoop, round slightly, and level with a case knife, care being taken not to shake the cup.*

While this may seem obvious to us now, the level measure was revolutionary and, while not as precise as measuring ingredients by weight, allowed anyone with a measuring cup and a teaspoon to cook from her book.

continues

Vinegar Candy

continued

2 cups (400 g) superfine sugar

½ cup (120 ml) apple cider vinegar

2 tablespoons (30 g) salted butter (plus more for buttering the pan and pulling the taffy)

Pinch of kosher salt

At a time when domestic cooks were becoming rare, it allowed the average housewife to create excellent meals for her family. In subsequent decades, Fannie Farmer's cookbook even became known as "The Bride's Bible," and in 1947 an article in the *Boston Globe* described Ms. Farmer as "the New England spinster school ma'am who taught millions of women the way to a man's heart.' It was a different time.

Thanks to Fannie Farmer's well-written recipes, I've had to do very little updating when adding this one to this book. Just remember when you measure the sugar to level it off, just as Ms. Farmer taught us.

MAKES 30 CANDIES   **COOK TIME:** 1 HOUR 45 MINUTES

1. Generously butter a large baking dish or several plates and set aside.

2. In a large saucepan, combine the sugar, apple cider vinegar, 2 tablespoons butter, and salt and mix together. Set over medium heat, stirring occasionally, until sugar is melted. A heatproof silicon spatula is best for stirring. Once the mixture comes to a boil, do not stir any longer. Let the mixture boil until it reaches the hard ball stage, 250°F to 265°F (120°C to 130°C) on a candy thermometer, or when a small amount of the syrup dropped in cold water forms a ball. If it goes past this stage, it will still be workable but will end in a harder candy.

3. Once the candy reaches the hard ball stage, take it off the heat and pour it into the prepared baking dish and let it sit for 10 to 15 minutes, or until cool enough to handle. Do not let it cool too much or it will become difficult to pull.

4. Once the candy is cooled enough, take it out of the pan. If it sticks, you may need to pry it up with a butter knife. Coat your fingers in butter, then begin pulling and twisting the taffy between your hands, folding it over, then pulling again. The warm taffy will be an amber color. Continue pulling until it is matte white and becomes too hard to pull. This can take anywhere from 30 to 60 minutes, and it may be beneficial to have two people alternating the work when one's arms become too tired. Once the taffy becomes difficult to pull, twist it into a long rope and cut it into 1-inch candies. Wrap the candies in wax paper to keep them from sticking.

Raspberry Shrub

✕✕✕✕✕✕✕✕✕✕✕✕✕✕✕

City/Region: United States
of America
Time Period: 1911

FROM HISTORY

*Put one quart of ripe raspberries in a bowl,
add two cups of vinegar, mash the berries
slightly, and let stand overnight. In the morning,
scald and strain until clear. Measure, and to
each cup of juice add one cup of sugar, boil
twenty minutes and seal.*

—Rufus Estes, *Good Things to Eat, as Suggested by Rufus*

Rufus Estes

A vinegar-based drink might sound a little suspect at first glance, but they've been popular since at least Ancient Rome, where soldiers drank an energy drink called *posca*. Back then, it was just vinegar and water, so the addition of berries and sugar in more recent centuries should be welcome. The combination of sweet and sour creates a similar profile to the whiskey sour or even a tart lemon drop martini.

Recipes for shrub can be found in many cookbooks of the eighteenth and nineteenth centuries, but the source for this version is unique, as *Good Things to Eat, as Suggested by Rufus* was the first cookbook written by an African American chef. Rufus Estes was born into slavery in Tennessee in 1857, the youngest of nine children, seven boys and two girls:

> *After the war broke out all the male slaves in the
> neighborhood for miles around ran off and joined the
> "Yankees." This left us little folks to bear the burdens. At
> the age of five I had to carry water from the spring about a
> quarter of a mile from the house, drive the cows to and from
> the pastures, mind the calves, gather chips, etc.*

"Chips," in this case, referred not to potato chips, but to dried cow poop that could be gathered and burned as fuel. After this work I'm sure Rufus was champing at the bit for any other job, and after the war the family moved to Nashville, where, at sixteen, Rufus began work in a restaurant.

continues

Raspberry Shrub

continued

He proved himself an excellent cook and in 1881 was offered a lucrative job, at $10 a week, in Chicago, where he could pursue his passion for cooking. In no time, he secured a position on one of the prestigious Pullman cars, luxury train cars that catered to the wealthiest and most famous American figures of the late nineteenth century. Rufus called out a number of them in his cookbook including the African explorer Henry Morton Stanley, the princess of Spain, and Presidents Grover Cleveland and Benjamin Harrison. As a chef to America's elite, Rufus became something of a celebrity himself and by the end of the century was the head chef for the Illinois subsidiary of J. P. Morgan and Andrew Carnegie's United States Steel Corporation.

Having achieved acclaim as a chef, Rufus did as all celebrity chefs (or YouTube chefs) do and wrote a cookbook, the first copy of which was auctioned off for an astonishing $11, an estimated $350 today. The book mostly includes dishes that would have been served to the clientele he spent his life cooking for, but many have their roots in his earlier years. Recipes like his fried chicken, hominy muffins, and this recipe for raspberry shrub.

MAKES ABOUT 1 QUART   **COOK TIME:** 12 HOURS 45 MINUTES

1 quart (700 g) fresh ripe raspberries, washed

2 cups (475 ml) white wine vinegar

3 cups (600 g) granulated sugar

Sparkling water, if desired

1. Put the raspberries in a small saucepan with the white wine vinegar. Mash the berries enough so that there are no full berries left intact, but it does not need to be mashed to a puree. Cover the saucepan and let sit for 12 hours.

2. Once the berries have been infused into the vinegar, take the saucepan and set it over a medium heat, bringing it to a boil for 1 minute. Then remove it from the heat and pour the mixture through a sieve into a large saucepan. Add the sugar and whisk until dissolved, then set the pan over medium-low heat and bring to a simmer for 20 minutes, stirring occasionally to ensure all of the sugar has dissolved. Remove the shrub from the heat and let it cool completely before pouring it into a container to chill in the refrigerator.

3. Once chilled, the shrub can be drunk as is over ice or slightly diluted with sparkling water, if desired. It's also excellent mixed into a cocktail of white wine or another spirit.

Texas Pecan Pie

City/Region: Texas
Time Period: 1914

Pecan varieties

I love pecan pie, but often I find the corn syrup to pecan ratio way out of balance: a crust filled with corn syrup and a dusting of pecan on top. My answer to this is to ditch the corn syrup altogether by making this pecan pie from 1914, a time before corn syrup came to dominate the dessert. A golden age for the pecan.

The word "pecan" comes, via the French, from the Algonquin word *Paccan*, which referred to any nut that required a stone to crack. We can be glad that this is the name that stuck rather than what Spanish settlers dubbed them, *nuez de la arruga*, which translates to "wrinkle nut." I don't imagine many families would welcome a wrinkle nut pie at their Thanksgiving table.

For most of their history pecans grew wild, the first orchard not being planted until 1772 on Long Island, New York. It was around the time that the nut was becoming quite popular with America's founding fathers. Thomas Jefferson, who often called them Illinois nuts in his writings, gave a bag to George Washington, who had them planted at Mount Vernon, and the general was said to have always had his pockets filled with the nuts and was constantly eating them throughout the Revolution.

The problem with these early pecan orchards was that the nuts were inconsistent. One tree could produce delicious, sweet pecans and the one next to it would give a crop so bitter as to be inedible. As with many trees,

continues

Texas Pecan Pie

continued

grafting was the answer to this dilemma, but the pecan proved difficult to graft. There had been a few small successes in the early nineteenth century, but the most prosperous were the work of an enslaved gardener named Antoine at Oak Alley Plantation in Louisiana. In 1846 Antoine grafted sixteen trees and later another hundred, and in 1876, long after Antoine had left the historic record, the nuts from those trees won Best Pecan at the Philadelphia Centennial Exposition. They became known as Centennial Pecan trees and they produced the first commercially viable nut.

Surely, pecan pies had been made before this time, but it was with the Centennial Pecan that the country saw the beginning of the pecan craze. Hundreds of recipes for pies and other pecan-based dishes started to find their way into cookbooks, mostly from the Deep South and Texas. But it was in the 1930s that pecan pie made the leap to Thanksgiving tables all over the country when Karo Syrup started slapping a recipe for pecan pie on every bottle of their corn syrup and, of course, included their syrup as a major ingredient. And if a modern pie is made with just a bit of the syrup, I have no problem with it, but I must admit, for a true lover of pecans, this 1914 recipe will replace any other on your Thanksgiving table.

MAKES ONE 9-INCH PIE   **COOK TIME:** 2 HOURS

FOR THE CRUST:

½ cup (65 g) powdered sugar

½ cup (113 g) unsalted butter, chilled and cut into ½-inch cubes

3 or 4 large egg yolks

1 teaspoon pure vanilla extract

1¾ cups (238 g) all-purpose flour

Pinch of kosher salt

1. Make the crust: Sift powdered sugar into a bowl and add the cubed butter. Beat until smooth. Beat in the egg yolks one at a time. The mixture may look curdled at this point, but that is okay. Add the vanilla. Sift in the flour and salt and slowly mix until just combined into a loose, crumbly dough. If the dough is too crumbly to come together, add another egg yolk. Form the dough into a ball and place it between two sheets of parchment and roll into an 11-inch (28 cm) disk, ⅛ inch thick. Set the dough and parchment in the refrigerator to chill for 20 minutes. Using butter or nonstick cooking spray, lightly grease a 9-inch pie dish or tart tin.

2. Once the dough has chilled, remove it from the refrigerator and discard the parchment. Transfer the dough to the prepared pie dish and crimp the edges. Cover in aluminum foil and set it in the freezer for 20 minutes.

3. Preheat the oven to 425°F/215°C.

FOR THE FILLING (SEE COOK'S NOTE):
3 large eggs

1 cup (235 ml) whole milk

1 cup (220 g) dark brown sugar

1 tablespoon all-purpose flour

½ cup (70 g) finely chopped raw, unsalted pecans, plus chopped pecans or pecan halves for an extra layer of pecan, optional

Pinch of kosher salt

FOR THE MERINGUE:
2 large egg whites at room temperature

3 tablespoons baker's sugar

4. Remove the dish from the freezer and remove the aluminum foil. Prick the bottom of the crust all over with a fork, then use the aluminum foil to line the crust, making sure the foil covers the edges of the crust, and fill with pie weights. Set the dish on a baking sheet and bake on the lower-middle rack for 15 minutes. Remove the dish from the oven and, using oven mitts, quickly remove the pie weights and foil and return the empty crust to the oven for 7 minutes or until the bottom has dried and is golden brown. Remove the crust from the oven and allow to cool completely.

5. Reduce the oven temperature to 350°F/175°C.

6. Make the filling: Whisk the eggs in a medium saucepan, then whisk in the whole milk and brown sugar until smooth. Sift in the tablespoon of flour, then add the ½ cup chopped pecans and salt and whisk until combined. Set the saucepan over medium-low heat. Gently stirring throughout, heat the mixture until you see steam begin to rise. Continue to let it cook for 2 to 3 minutes, making sure it does not begin to simmer, then remove it from the heat and pour the filling into the cooled piecrust. If adding additional pecans, place them on top of the filling, then carefully set the pie in the oven and bake until there is just a slight wobble in the center, about 30 to 35 minutes. Then remove the pie from the oven and cool completely before adding the meringue.

7. Make the meringue: Make sure your bowl and beaters are clean and perfectly dry. Beat the egg whites in a large bowl at medium speed until you form soft, shiny peaks. Then beat at a high speed while slowly adding the sugar 1 tablespoon at a time. Continue to beat until you form shiny, stiff peaks. Then spread or pipe the meringue onto the pie and place it on the top rack of the oven, so that the meringue is about 4 inches away from the top of the oven. Bake at 350°F/175°C for 10 minutes, until the edges of the meringue are golden. Once the pie is baked, you can sprinkle on a few more chopped pecans as decoration, then serve.

Cook's Note: If you are using a deep pie pan instead of a tart tin, double the amount of filling.

Acknowledgments

First, I thank my husband, José, for supporting my idea to start a YouTube channel right from the beginning. When I was furloughed from work, instead of watching TV, he encouraged me to keep making videos. I would have never stuck with the channel or finished this book without his calming presence (along with that of our cats, Jaime and Cersei).

My family, for putting up with years of my saying, "Hey, did you know that . . . ?" And especially my grandpa, who first inspired my love of history and storytelling, and my mom and dad for exposing me to all sorts of cuisine, whether I liked it or not.

Maureen Grandchamp, for introducing me to *The Great British Bake Off* and Mary Berry. It was Mary Berry's master classes that inspired me to get into the kitchen and learn how to bake. Thank you to Anja Schmidt for bringing me the opportunity to write this book and to Justin Schwartz and the team at Simon & Schuster for helping me to see it through.

Ann Volkwein, who took my convoluted cooking instructions and crafted them into the beautiful recipes in this book. Her enthusiasm for this project kept me going throughout.

Etrigan and all of my Patreon patrons who have supported me through this process and especially to those who gave up their weekends to test these recipes and give me invaluable feedback.

Everyone who helped with translating and deciphering old texts and recipes. There would be no cookbook without the help of Ken Albala, Gojko Barjamovic, Tova Äng, Francesco Vitellini, Roy Chan, Joshua and Ellen Badgley, Nawal Nasrallah, Rich Oh, Susanna Monteros, Glenn Gorsuch, Jacki Murphy, and Ellie Homard-Roy.

My manager, Jeremy Katz, for spending countless hours finding and clearing images, finding the mistakes I so often miss, and basically every other task I've ever asked him to do. And my agents, Jim Stein and Marla Haut, who are my constant advocates in everything I do.

The photographer, Andrew Bui, and his team for making these dishes look far better than I could have ever hoped or been able to do myself.

My family at Walt Disney Studios who listened to me prattle on about food history and who tested many of my first historic dishes. They also supported my not returning to work so I could focus on *Tasting History* full time.

A huge thank-you to all of you wonderful fellow food history nerds who have come before me and made what I do possible. The SCA and other groups who devote their life to keeping the past alive have done so much of the heavy lifting when it comes to research throughout the years.

And finally, thank you to everyone who watches *Tasting History with Max Miller* each week. You are the reason this book was written, and you are the reason I'm excited to get up each morning and get to work.

Image Credits

All artworks in the book are faithful photographic reproductions of two-dimensional, public-domain works of art, and the artworks themselves are in the public domain in the United States except as follows:

Permissions & Sources

Stew of Lamb, Babylon, c. 1740 BC
1. Gojko Barjamovic et al., *The Yale Babylonian Tablets*, last modified June 11, 2019, https://www.laphamsquarterly.org/roundtable/ancient-mesopotamian-tablet-cookbook.

Tuh'u, Babylon, c. 1740 BC
1. Barjamovic, et al., *Tablets.*
2. Stephanie Dalley, *Myths from Mesopotamia: Creation, the Flood, Gilgamesh, and Others*, rev. ed. (Oxford: Oxford University Press, 2009), 253–54.

Melas Zomos (Spartan Black Broth), Sparta, c. 400 BC
1. Plutarch, *Moralia, in Fifteen Volumes, with an English Translation by Frank Cole Babbitt*, trans. Frank Cole Babbitt (Cambridge, MA: Harvard University Press, 1931).
2. Athenaeus, *The Deipnosophists*, Loeb Classical Library Edition, trans. Charles Burton Gulick (Cambridge: Harvard University Press, 1957).
3. Ibid.

Epityrum, The Roman Republic, c. 160 BC
1. Cato the Elder, *De agri cultura*, Loeb Classical Library Edition, trans. W. D. Hooper and H. B. Ash (Cambridge, MA: Harvard University Press, 1934).

Globi, The Roman Republic, c. 160 BC
1. Cato the Elder, *De agri cultura.*
2. Marcus Valerius Martialis, *Martial: The Twelve Books of Epigrams*, trans. J.A. Pott, M.A. and F.A. Wright (London: George Routledge & Sons Ltd., 1924).

Placenta, The Roman Republic, c. 160 BC
1. Cato the Elder, *De agricultura.*
2. Cato the Elder, *De agricultura.*

Puls, The Roman Empire, c. 2nd century
1. Galen, *Galen: On the Properties of Foodstuffs*, trans. Owen Powell (Cambridge: Cambridge University Press, 2003), 59.
2. Silius Italicus, *Punica*, trans. J.D. Duff (London: William Heinemann Ltd.,1934).

Pullum Parthicum (Parthian Chicken), The Roman Empire, c. 1st to 4th century
1. John E. Hill, *Through the Jade Gate to Rome: A Study of the Silk Routes during the Later Han Dynasty, 1st to 2nd Centuries CE* (Charleston, SC: Booksurge Publishing, 2009), 23.

Vitellian Piglet, The Roman Empire, 1st to 4th century
1. Cassius Dio, *Roman History*, vol. VIII, trans. Earnest Cary (Cambridge, MA: Harvard University Press, 1925), 225.

Crustade Lombarde, England, c. 1450
1. Benedict of Nursia, *St. Benedict's Rule for Monasteries*, trans. Leonard J. Doyle (Collegeville, MN: The Liturgical Press, 1950).

Soul Cakes, England, c. 1600
1. Hilary Spurling, *Elinor Fettiplace's Receipt Book* (New York: Viking Publishing, 1986).

Stobhach Gaedhealach (Irish Stew), Ireland, c. 1900
1. Sisters of Mercy, *Leabhar cócaireachta*, trans. Jacki Murphy (1900).

Torta d'Herbe Communi, Italy, 1570
1. Bartolomeo Scappi, *The Opera of Bartolomeo Scappi (1570): L'arte et prudenza d'un maestro Cuoco (The Art and Craft of a Master Cook)*, trans. Terence Scully (Toronto: University of Toronto Press, 2008), 99, 103, 481, 484.
2. Ibid.
3. Ibid.

Pumpkin Tourte, Italy, 1570
1. Scappi, *Opera dell'arte*

Beef with Garlic Harvester Sauce, Transylvania, 1580
1. Glenn Gorsuch, "The Prince of Transylvania's Court Cookbook", trans. Bence Kovacs, last modified 2018, http://www.fibergeek.com/leathernotebook/the-transylvanian-cookbook/.

Cannetons de Roüen à l'échalote (Rouen Duck with Shallots), France, 1739
1. Jean Anthelme Brillat-Savarin, *The Physiology of Taste*, trans. M.F.K. Fisher (New York: Alfred A. Knopf, 1825).

Semlor (Hettwägg med mandel), Sweden, 1755
1. Cajsa Warg, *Hjelpreda i hushållningen för unga fruentimber*, trans. by Tova Äng.
2. Herman Schützercrantz, *The Misfortunes of Swedish Kings*, trans. by Tova Äng (1775).

Pomodori Farciti all'Erbette, Italy, 1773
1. Vincenzo Corrado, *Il cuoco galante*, trans. Francesco Vitellini.
2. Miles Kington, "Heading for a sticky end," *The Independent*, last modified March 28, 2003, https://www.independent.co.uk/voices/columnists/miles-kington/heading-for-a-sticky-end-112674.html.

La Pêche Melba, France/England, 1903
1. Auguste Escoffier, *Auguste Escoffier: Memories of my Life*, trans. Laurence Escoffier (Hoboken, NJ: Wiley, 1996).

Payasam, India, c. 12th century
1. *Royal Life in Mānasollāsa*, trans. P. Arundhati (Sundeep Prakashan, 1994).

Niangao, China, 544
1. Jia Sixie, *Qímín yāoshù*, trans. Roy Chan.

Yuanxiao, Ming China, 1620s
1. Liu Ruoyu, *Zhuo zhong zhi*, trans. Roy Chan.

Nyumen, Japan, 1643
1. *Ryori Monogatari*, trans. Joshua Badgley, https://sengokudaimyo.com.

Little Meat Cakes, Chinese Mongol Empire, c. 1330
1. Paul D. Buell and E.N. Anderson, *A Soup for the Qan: Chinese Dietary Medicine of the Mongol Era as Seen in Hu Sihui's Yinshan Zhengyao: Introduction, Translation, Commentary, and Chinese Text. Second Revised and Expanded Edition* (Leiden: Brill, 2010), 37, 307.
2. Buell and Anderson, *A Soup for the Qan*.

Makshufa, Baghdad, c. 13th century
1. Muhammad b.al-Husan, *A Baghdad Cookery Book*, trans. Charles Perry (Totnes, UK: Prospect Books, 2005).

Hummus Kassa, Egypt, c. 14th century
1. *Treasure Trove of Benefits and Variety at the Table*, trans. Nasrallah Nawal (Leiden: Brill, 2017), 381, 382.
2. Ibid.
3. Ibid.

Tamales, Mexico, c. 1520
1. Bernardino de Sahagún, *Florentine Codex: General History of the Things of New Spain*, trans. Arthur J.O. Anderson and Charles E. Dibble (Salt Lake City: University of Utah Press, 1970).

Aztec Chocolate, Mexico, c. 1520
1. Bernardino de Sahagún, *General History of the Things of New Spain* (Santa Fe, NM: School of American Research), quoted in Sophie D. Coe, *America's First Cuisines* (Austin: University of Texas Press, 1994).